Michael O'Kane

Doing Business in Myanmar

Andalus Publishing 2014, 2018

Doing Business in Myanmar
©2014 Andalus Publishing
ISBN-13: 978-1-945979-00-2, E-book: 978-1-945979-01-9

Publisher's Cataloging-In-Publication Data

O'Kane, Michael, 1955–
    Doing business in Myanmar / Michael O'Kane.
    Chicago : Andalus Publishing, c2014.

    p. ; cm.

    Includes bibliography and index.
    ISBN: 978-1-945979-00-2 E-book: 978-1-945979-01-9

    Summary: A general introduction to doing business in Myanmar, covering all aspects of commercial and private law containing a brief historical background and review of the country's economy, corporate and commercial requirements, banking regulations, corporate set-up rules as well as an overview of the legal system. –Publisher.

    1. Commercial law–Burma. 2. Investments, Foreign–Burma. 3. Foreign trade regulation–Burma. 4. Business enterprises–Law and legislation–Burma. 5. Corporation law–Burma. 6. Banking law–Burma. 7. Real property–Law and legislation–Burma. 8. Dispute resolution–Burma. I. Title.

KNL856.053 2014

346.591–dc23   2015

Contents

CHAPTER 1

At a Glance

Official name: The Republic of the Union of Myanmar (as adopted in 1989)
Status: Independent from the UK (since 1948)
Location: In Southeast Asia
Geographic coordinates: 22 00 N, 98 00 E
Neigboring countries: Bangladesh, China, India, Laos and Thailand
Area: 676,577 sq km - the largest country in mainland Southeast Asia
Access to sea: Approximately 3,000 km of coastline on the Bay of Bengal & the Andaman Sea
Climate: tropical monsoon; cloudy, rainy, hot, humid summers (southwest monsoon, June to September); less cloudy, scant rainfall, mild temperatures, lower humidity during winter (northeast monsoon, December to April)
Terrain: central lowlands ringed by steep, rugged highlands
Capital: Nay Pyi Taw
National holiday: Independence Day, 4 January

(1948)

Population: 51.4 million (2015 census)

Ethnic groups: Burman 68%, Shan 9%, Karen 7%, Rakhine 4%, Chinese 3%, Mon 2%, Indian 2%, other 5%

Religions: Buddhist 89%, Christian 4% (Baptist 3%, Roman Catholic 1%), Muslim 4%, animist beliefs 1%, other 2%

Literacy: Approx. 90%

Density: 85 people per sq. km

Language: Myanmar and English

Currency: 1 kyat (K) = 100 pyas

GDP in 2015: $283.5 billion USD$

GDP per capita in 2015   :5,500 (5x increase over 2013)

GDP growth in 2015: 7%

International phone code: +95

Internet country code: .mm

Civil aircraft registration code: XY

Time zone: GMT +6hr 30min

CHAPTER 2

Introduction

THIS REPORT IS OUT OF DATE. In Myanmar, each new day brings significant change.

First a medieval kingdom, then a prosperous British colony, and then an occupied wartime territory, followed by brief independence and fifty years as a pariah state, Myanmar is rapidly moving to once again take its place amongst world nations. Myanmar has embarked upon an aggressive economic modernization program that promises to bring real change to the country. The pace of change is breathtaking: new laws are written and old ones are revived. Construction projects are planned, awarded and are underway at a ferocious clip. Construction of a new international terminal at the Yangon International Airport has been completed; work continues on a new domestic terminal. Under the military regime, contact with the outside world was viewed suspiciously. Foreigners were monitored and citizens were under the obligation to report any contact. To protect themselves, citizens began avoiding any foreigner. Today foreign investment is actively courted.

The era of sanctions is over and new trade partners seek business introductions. Even English has been restored as a language of instruction.

Myanmar is both the poorest and largest country of Southeast Asia. Approximately 32% of the population lives in poverty. Myanmar borders Bangladesh and India to the West, China to the North and Northeast, Laos to the East and Thailand to the East and south. The country consists of seven separate states and seven regions. The Republic of the Union of Myanmar, as its official name suggests, is not simply one nation. The country is a collection of many ethnicities, each with its own language and customs. Myanmar is a unitary, presidential and constitutional republic. Since 2016, Htin Kyaw is the elected head of state, but see the discussion below.

In 2011 the military regime formally transferred power to a civilian government. Nevertheless, under the current constitution there is a separate system of military courts and the military retains the right to make appointments to government offices.

Myanmar is extraordinarily diverse. There are over 135 recognized ethnic groups, ranging from the (former) headhunting clans of Naga warriors to the majority Burmese. Some Burmese states, or divisions, continue to seek independence, sometimes violently. One of them, the Karen, is predominantly Christian. In World War II their nascent army was trained by the American military detailed to the forerunner of the Central Intelligence Agency. The Karen have long sought independence and still have their own army though a truce is now in place. Though Burmese and English predominate, sixty-seven different languages are spoken in the Union.

Even the name of the country is controversial. The word "Burma" is so established in English that many resist change. The United States does not officially recognize the new name, Myanmar. It is not clear how much significance can be given to these naming conventions. In the past fifty years, the name of the country's highest judicial body has changed three times.

Yangon is the Burmese name for the country's largest city and former capital, founded in 1755. The city was built on the site of an ancient city called Ramanago in 746 by King Arammanaraza. Afterwards the name was corrupted to *Dagone*. The city became a refuge for those fleeing their debts in India. Enforcement of the laws was lax, for the city was "crowded with foreigners of desperate fortunes, who supported themselves by petty trade."[1]

Yangon is located in the southern part of the country on the east bank of the Irrawaddy River, forty kilometers north of the Gulf of Martaban of the Andaman Sea. In 1989 the government formally asked that other countries call the city Yangon, but the British Embassy in Yangon continues to call the former capital city by

---

[1] Sangermano, Fr. Vincenzo, *The Burmese Empire a Hundred Years Ago* (1833)(3rd. ed. 1893)

its English name, Rangoon. Yangon is the largest city in Myanmar. In 2006, the government established a new inland capital, called Nay Pyi Taw (Naypyidaw).

The first European to visit Burma was Marco Polo in the 13th century. British influence in the various areas of what is now Myanmar ebbed and flowed until 1862 when British Burma was designated a new province of British India. On January 1, 1886, Britain overthrew King Theebaw and annexed the Kindom of Burma at the end of the Third Burmese War. For the next fifty years, Burma was primarily ruled as a part of India.

From 1885 to 1948 Burma was a British colony. By the time the country came under British control Christian missionaries had already made significant inroads and had for all practical purposes converted the Karen. Administratively, Burma was part of British India until 1935 and British Indian law was applied.

In 1935, passage of the Government of Burma Act removed Burma from colonial administration under India and gave Burma its own constitution, but not independence. The constitution took effect on April 1, 1937 and provided for a bicameral legislature with an elected House of Representatives. The Governor was required to obey the legislature except in matters of defense, foreign relations and monetary policy. Ultimately the Governor answered to the authority of the British Parliament. After the Japanese invasion in 1942, the Burmese government was suspended and only resumed power in October 1945 after a short period of military governance following the defeat of the Japanese. Three years later, on January 4, 1948, Burma became an independent republic.

But Burma had always been considered a separate jurisdiction. In the 1930's the winds of change were upon Southeast Asia. Thailand had become a constitutional monarchy. Independence movements were stirring in both the French and British colonies. The 268-year-old Qing dynasty had fallen and China was now a republic. Burma was not untouched. Burmese leaders lobbied for autonomy. After the Japanese invaded in 1941, General Aung San (father of Nobel Peace Prize winner Aung San Suu Kyi) formed the Burmese Independence Army. The Army at first allied itself with the Japanese invaders, but later became disillusioned and switched sides. Lord Mountbatten convinced the British to forgive, stating that the Japanese had tricked the young Burmese fighters who were anxious for independence. It is unclear whether this was an act of generosity or the recognition of postwar political reality. The wartime guide for British servicemen somewhat bitterly stated,

> "The Japanese made enormous capital out of the relatively small fifth column they used in 1942. Don't help them now by believing every Burmese is against us."[2]

2 *A Pocket Guide to Burma*, British Army, 1945.

In the end, the British Government ignored the flirtation with the Japanese invaders and on January 4, 1948 the country won its independence. Independent Burma did not join the Commonwealth. Not all the regions of the country were happy with the terms of independence. Many in Shan State, who are ethnically Thai, felt betrayed by the British who, it is alleged, promised them a separate country. Under Article 201 of the 1947 Constitution, any state had the option to secede from the Union after a period of ten years. Both the 1974 and 2008 constitutions prohibit secession. After the military coup of 1962, secession was unlikely to be achieved by peaceful means.

The fighting that began with the Japanese invasion in 1941 has not ended. The Karen National Union, the Shan State Army and the Kachin Independence Organization have at various times each been involved in armed conflict with the Burmese Army, the *Tatmadaw*. As in many other countries, the issue is religion. In addition to the Muslim religous minority, the Karen, a predominantly Christian ethnic group, are predominantly Christian and consider themselves separate from the Burmese. Their desire for a state of their own has caused them to take up arms several times since 1948 in order to accomplish this goal.

These states are rich in natural resources and the government's control over them was tenuous at best. The Shan and Karen states have abundant teak forests. When logging was banned in Thailand, the Union gov-

ernment permitted Thai logging companies to negotiate with the Shan and Karen authorities for permission
to engage in logging activities. Though the situation
is different today, Shan State officials look to the oil
pipeline crossing their territory into China as a potential source of revenue. For years, at least a quarter of
the country was under the control of one or more of
these rebel groups.

In 1962 the military staged a coup and the country became a socialist state. In the two decades after
the coup, rebel armies and warlords were active in the
country. One year after Burmese independence, the
remnants of the 93rd Division of the Chinese nationalist army fled into Burma, specifically, Shan State. This
army aligned itself with Shan and other independence
groups. With the protection of the warlords, opium
cultivation became an important cash crop for the
rebels. One of these warlords, Khun Sa, who had been
trained by Kuomintang remnants, became the world's
largest heroin trafficker while leading a 12,000 man-
strong army and covertly maintaining relations with the
United States. Though one of the world's largest heroin
producers, Khun Sa claimed to be a Shan nationalist
and a freedom fighter.

His area of operations was a no-go zone for the
Burmese Army and became known as the Golden Tri-
angle. The Burmese government captured him in 1969;
in 1973 his army captured two Russian doctors and demanded that he be freed in exchange for their release.

He offered to sell his entire crop to the Australian and U.S. governments. Both governments rejected the offer, even though it would have practically made heroin unavailable.

After the U.S. refused his offer to leave the drug trade, he was indicted in New York on drug trafficking charges. He surrendered to the Burmese Army, which then refused to extradite him. The U.S. Drug Enforcement Administration unsuccessfully attempted to have him murdered but the attempt failed. In 1975 Saigon fell and the United States wanted nothing more to do with Southeast Asia.

In 1988, student demonstrations led to a three-year closing of the universities but eventually caused the government to take tentative steps towards reform. The military government rebooted itself and became known as the State Law and Order Restoration Council.

In May 1990 national parliamentary elections were held. The National League for Democracy Party, headed by Aung San Suu Kyi, won the elections but the State Law and Order Restoration Council failed to honor the election results. Oppressive government policies remained in place until a civilian government took control in 2010. Thereafter, economic reform was announced as the country's official policy and the pace of change accelerated.

In November, 2015, Aung San Suu Kyi's National League for Democracy party won a majority of seats in Myanmar's parliament. The Myanmar constitution, in a provision that was written specifically to keep her from being elected president, prohibits those with foreign spouses or foreign passport holding children from taking the high office. The NLD named Aung San Suu Kyi a state councillor while naming a lieutenant, Htin Kyaw, to the presidency, thus handily side-stepping the constitutional prohibition.

Despite the election, the Army controls 25% of the seats in parliament and has control over the crucial ministries of the interior, defense and border affairs. More importantly, the Army has respected the will of the electorate. Accepting the results of the election has directly led to the elimination of foreign sanctions against Myanmar.

Excitement over the election results and the military's decision to respect them must nevertheless be treated with caution. The military situation in the country is dynamic. Not all of the local armies have disarmed. Some truces hold, while others are apt to flare up at any moment.

The situation of the Rohingya Muslim population continues to be in flux, with one million persons denied full citizenship in the Union. Myanmar considers them illegal immigrants from India and calls them "Bengali"despite their presence in Burmese territory for generations. Buddhist monks have led demonstrations against their presence in the country. Burma is 90% Buddhist and the monks claim that the Muslims will change the essential nature of the country. The

Rohingya are officially considered illegal immigrants and thus, stateless persons. In November, 2016 a Rohingya attack on a government police station resulted in the deaths of several policemen, a harsh government response and the now-familiar flotillas of boat people seeking refuge, this time in Bangladesh. But Bangladesh, a poor country, does not want to accept the Rohingya either.

The issue of how to deal with the Muslim minority was so intractable for India at the time of negotiations with Britain for the end of colonialism that the only acceptable solution was partition, with what had been British India split into majority-Hindu India and majority-Muslim Pakistan. At the time of Burmese independence, the issue of the status of the Muslim Rohingya minority in Rakhine state was not addressed. Because Burma had been part of India, there was large Indian community resident in Burma at the time of independence. In 1962, the revolutionary government forced the expropriation of Indian businesses and the deportation of Burmese Indians. Over 400,000 left. As a consequence, the government treats those Indian Muslims who stayed as illegal immigrants and not part of the nation. There is a systematic deprivation of their civil rights. It is unclear what kind of solution could be drafted that would satisfy both sides. Increasingly, the world community is taking notice. Accurate news, difficult to come by in this Internet age of unverified news, is especially difficult to obtain from Rakhine state. After military operations were announced in response to the attack, Rakhine state was declared an off-limits military zone making accurate reporting difficult.

The human rights situation and the struggle for democracy have long captured world attention. Others have written eloquently about these issues and the struggle to restore democracy. The situation on the ground is changing so fast it is not at all clear that past paradigms mean much for the future.

Myanmar has seen exciting growth and liberalization of the economy since 2010. The country's development is proceeding at a frenetic pace and quite frankly it is an exciting place to be.

Nevertheless, there is reason for caution.

According to Kyaw Lin Oo, coordinator of the Myanmar People's Forum,

> "Many local business people are afraid of the Asian Economic Community. They assume it will threaten them, as multinational corporations will enter our country with better quality goods and more reasonable prices."[3]

If you open your markets too far, some will want to close them.

Burma was one of the founding members of GATT, the General Agreement of Tariffs and Trade, the orga-

[3]"Getting Ready for the Major League", Nyeinchan Win and Thet Mon Htun, *Eleven Media* (Myanmar) December 13, 2013

nization that eventually became the World Trade Organization. During the socialist period, membership was allowed to lapse. Since 1995 Myanmar has been a member of the WTO and this means additional worries about foreign competition affecting local business.

The last reliable census was taken in the 1930's and the records were destroyed during the Japanese invasion. In 2014, the government completed a controversial census. The working figure, prior to the census, was 61.57 million people based on the return of government forms. The final results of the census showed a population of 51.4 million, well below this estimate. Approximately 1.2 million people in Rakhine, Kachin and Kayin States were not counted. As in other nations, the census itself had become more than just a counting exercise.

There is no official category in the census for "Rohingya" despite the fact that 135 other ethnic minorities are recognized. Ye Htut, a government spokesman said, "We will not register people who say they are Rohingya."[4]

Recent business articles about Myanmar have tended to focus on current events while ignoring the country's rich history. Other books focus on the political and human rights situation to the exclusion of all other topics. Historical works are useful for the understanding of the country's current business and legal structure. After all, the British Companies Law of

---

[4] *The Nation*, Bangkok, March 31 2014

1914, while no longer the law in the United Kingdom, is still the law in the Union of Myanmar.[5] Though to be fair, a new companies law has been proposed and is expected to be passed in 2016. The draft text is treated extensively in this book.

Pre-liberalization works describe a drastic, oppressive surveillance state with little access to the outside world and secret spies run amok amidst a citizenry afraid to speak out.

While some still live in fear, the Myanmar of today is not the Myanmar of ten or fifteen years ago. Whether due to international political activism or other causes, business in Myanmar has been liberalized. In writing this business guide, my intent is not to ignore the noble work of those who have suffered in order to bring change to their country. Others have written about these matters extensively and eloquently. What is needed is a short text that accurately reflects today's more favorable business climate.

This book attempts to bridge the gap with a review of the current business environment based on an understanding of the historic business and legal environment. Research was conducted in Myanmar in 2013 and again in 2016. The author would like to ac-

---

[5]The title of this law is "The Burma Companies Act [India Act VII, 1913](1st April, 1914). However, a footnote to the law refers to it as [t]he Indian Companies, Act, 1913. In Myanmar today the 1914 date is commonly used even though the law dates from 1913.

knowledge and thank the research staff at the Charles
E. Young Research Library at the University of Cali-
fornia, Los Angeles for assistance provided.

CHAPTER 3

General

You might think you were traveling backwards in time, to a magical land of Kipling and pagodas. Flying into Burma you can see rice paddies and a dual-track narrow gauge railway that encircles Rangoon. Before coming to Myanmar I had spent a good deal of time reading about the country. But my preparation for Myanmar was not so much a historical survey as a collection of warnings.

I was warned that Burma is "different,"and that coming to the country would bring with it difficulties found in no other place. I was told to read Emma Larkin's book about Orwell. In *Finding George Orwell in Burma*, Larkin wrote of a terrible Stalinist surveillance state and lamented the demise of old Burma. She reported the police surveillance of herself and others, the censorship of newspapers, the secret police, the unjust incarcerations and the palpable fear she felt amongst the populace. "In Burma,"she wrote, "prison exists as an ever present underworld into which anyone can fall at any time."[1]

I was advised to take a flashlight so that I could walk the streets safely at night since reliable electricity was uncommon.

Before 1988 Burma was a grim place. There were no theaters, nightclubs or pubs. Supermarkets, shopping malls and amusement parks were similarly nonexistent. After the riots in 1988 the military shut the few remaining cinemas. Tourists could only obtain one-week visas. Contact with foreigners was restricted; Burmese were supposed to report any foreign contact to the police and their interaction with locals was carefully monitored by the secret police. Not since the days of the Venetian Republic and its official inquisitors had contact with foreigners been so circumscribed.

But Burma has always been a fantastical place:

> "The city was fantastic. The men wore pink silk wound round their heads. Everywhere one saw rose-colour. I bought toothpaste at a very grand chemist's shop in the shadow of the Gold Pagoda. King Cobras would wriggle across the road, and heave horribly under the rubbish heaps. You would meet strange Tibetans, dressed like shepherds from the Winter's Tale, and

---

[1] Larkin, *Finding George Orwell in Burma*, Penguin 2004, 2011

in the lifts of department stores you would find shorn Buddhist priests wearing the yellow robe."[2]

Burma has never been far from the magical. Astrology and black magic play important roles in the political realm. Fortunetellers are famous in Burma. During the recent Thai political troubles, it was front-page news that the ex-wife of the previous Prime Minister, Thaksin Shinawatra, had traveled to Myanmar to consult with San Zarni Bo, a famous fortuneteller. Bangkok's *The Nation* newspaper noted that many politicians, both Thai and Burmese, regularly sought his guidance. While there might be a tendency to discount these beliefs, an acquaintance with them is important for understanding the country today. In 1987, an astrologer advised former President Ne Win to change the denomination of the currency. One hundred and 50 kyat notes were discontinued in favor of 90 and 45 note denominations. The citizens turned to a review of their multiplication tables for multiples of the number nine. Fortunately, today these notes are no longer in use. In 1970 another astrologer advised that the country needed to change from driving on the left to driving on

---

[2]*Rangoon*, January 1941, by Silvia Baker (1947) reprinted in *Shades of Gold and Green, Anecdotes of Colonial Burmah 1886-1948*, compiled by Nicholas Greenwood, Asian Educational Services, New Delhi 1998.

the right. While the change was implemented, automobiles continued to be imported with the steering wheel on the right side of the car. The result, which continues today, is automobiles with right-side steering driving on the right. Left turns are a harrowing experience since the driver cannot see oncoming traffic without edging into it. Apparently the astrologer had not foreseen these complications. In the years since drivers have been using vehicles manufactured for a system not in effect in their country. Reform has so far been unsuccessful. A proposal to ban the importation of left-hand steering wheel vehicles is on hold with drivers arguing that the need to rubber-neck while making turns has made Myanmar drivers safer due to their increased agility.

Myanmar does not have a seven-day week. Instead, an eight-day week is used. The eighth day is created by splitting Wednesday, which then becomes two "days" of only twelve hours each. The second part of Wednesday runs from midday to midnight and is called *yahu*. Forms of address in Burmese include "U"for "Mr."and "Daw"for "Ms". or "Mrs."

Despite Myanmar's vast amounts of natural resources including 40,000 megawatts of clean hydropower potential and 481 billion cubic meters of proven natural gas reserves there are rolling brownouts and power cuts. The State-owned Myanmar Electric Power Enterprise (MEPE) has pledged to improve infrastructure and increase its electricity-generating capacity.

The reality is improving. Though many businesses in Rangoon still have their own power generators, as electrical generation becomes more reliable they are used less and less. In any event, I experienced no power cuts at all during my stay. I never had to use the flashlight. Even electric plugs are becoming standardized, though alongside the British three-pronged fused plug outlet you will sometimes find the Thai-style combo flat-round version as well.

Like the United States, Burma is one of three countries that have not generally adopted the metric system. However, in October 2013 the government announced that it would be adopting the metric system, leaving the U.S. and Liberia in a club of only two members.

Business and tourist visas are now easily obtained and the one-week limitation is gone. Tourist visas are available upon arrival in Myanmar. Tourist visas are valid for 28 days. The new Foreign Investment Law defines a range of activities that do not constitute "doing business"in the country, such as attending meetings. So if you need to go to Myanmar for a business meeting, you do not need a business visa. A regular business visa is available for a period of up to 70 days. A foreigner who needs to stay longer in Myanmar must apply for a Foreigner's Registration Certificate with one year's validity. The Permanent Residence of Foreigners Rules were issued in 2014.[3] The secret police no longer fol-

[3]*Doing Business in Myanmar*, Myanmar Legal Services Ltd., 9 September 2015

low foreigners around nor monitors their contacts with local businessmen. Guidebooks more than two years old will advise the traveler to take brand-new, crisp U.S. currency since ATM machines are not be connected to the international banking network. This is no longer the case. The elimination of economic sanctions has meant that Myanmar is now solidly connected to international financial networks. You will have no difficulty accessing your foreign account from a Myanmar ATM. There are many ATM's in the country and even a few inside the Schwedagon Pagoda. Taxis that once demanded payment in dollars now happily accept kyat, though this happiness may have less to do with the faith in the national currency than the restrictions imposed in 2015 by the Central Bank. The Union leapfrogged the goal of universal landline telephone service by granting Telenor of Norway and Ooredoo of Qatar licenses to provide mobile communications. GSM mobile phones work in the country and SIM cards can be obtained locally. Today the visitor will see few wired telephones set up on small tables on the sidewalk selling telephone calls to those who do not possess landlines. Mobile phones are now ubiquitous. Expected growth in the telecom sector means that such services will become a thing of the past.

During the years of military censorship, the Internet was not available. As recently as just a few years ago Internet service was stuck in the early 1990's: it was possible to check e-mails but not much else. Reliable Internet service has now been rolled out. There are Internet cafés in Rangoon and elsewhere; wireless is often available. Accommodation is still an issue but is greatly improved. Some guidebooks breathlessly report the difficulty of finding good lodging in Yangon as if this were breaking news. Rack rates at Manhattan levels may be evidence of a gold rush, but the lack of hotels in Burma is old news indeed. In 1927 one visitor noted:

> "The shortage of hotel accommo-
> dation operates against the prosperity
> of Rangoon, especially during October,
> when many visitors come from the east of
> India for their short annual holiday. Many
> of them are unable to stay in Rangoon
> merely because there is literally nowhere
> for them to sleep."[4]

Another visitor noted in 1941:

> "My hotel at Rangoon was a place of
> decayed splendour, pervaded by an over-
> powering smell of cat. As a matter of fact,
> in addition to the army of ordinary cats that
> lived there, there were a number of civet
> cats who haunted the rafters and raced

[4] Brown, A.Claude, The Land of Courtesy and Colour (1927)

> about all night...Hotels are not numerous,
> and the largest of them is situated two
> miles from the town. There is ample room
> for more hotels, but I am told it is none too
> easy to obtain a license."[5]

The government now allows wholly owned foreign companies to build three star hotels and above. The industry responded quickly. The hotel room shortage of just a few years ago is a thing of the past.Because of the shortage of higher-class hotels, international companies are building hotels as fast as they can to be able to profit from $300+ rack rates. As a result, a growing oversupply has caused prices to drop. The Parkroyal Hotel, a Singapore-based chain, has been open for some time. There is a Sofitel and a Novotel now in Yangon. Other chains are getting involved. There are plans to convert the old Burma Railway Company headquarters, a world heritage site, into a Peninsula Hotel.

W. Song, a hotelier in Yangon, says that the lack of hotels is due to the fact that during the period of the socialist government, private individuals were forbidden from building hotels. His company converted the compound of the former Yugoslavian Embassy into a hotel. The hotel, known as the Queen Shin Saw Pu Hotel, is a three star hotel on Windsor Road, an area between the city center and the airport. A room there will cost $50/night. There are several other hotels on

---

[5] Rangoon, January 1941, Id. at 134.

that street. Most hotels are one-star hotels and in the city center, these predominate. They can be a little forbidding, but one recommended hotel is the Mayfair Inn, at No. 57 38th Street (between Merchant Street and Strand Road). A single room at the Mayfair will set you back $20; a double $30. Both come with their own shower.

Leaving Burma presents no particular difficulties. Bags are X-rayed upon arrival at the airport, prior to checking in. Other than that initial inspection, leaving the country today is much like leaving any other. The new terminal now sports a luxury shopping mall and several fast food establishment offering Burmese, Thai, American and Chinese cuisine.

CHAPTER 4

The Economy

MYANMAR IS BLESSED WITH ABUNDANT NATURAL resources. Currently, hydrocarbons, mining and timber are the most productive segments of Myanmars economy. In 1962, Myanmar was the world's largest rice exporter, but the industry was allowed to languish under the military regime. At that time, the revolutionary government officially rejected foreign capitalism and adopted a Soviet-style centrally planned economy which it called the "Burmese Way to Socialism". The 1974 Constitution proclaimed a Socialist Republic and there was no doubt then what these words meant.

The 1974 Constitution similarly proclaimed that a "socialist society is the goal of the State" and that the economic system of the country is a "socialist economic system". Communist revolutions triumphed in Cambodia, Viet Nam and Laos in 1975; the Union was to follow them along an ill-defined "Burmese path" to a planned state economy.

Consequently, the economy suffered. At least a third of the national budget was dedicated to military needs. Consumer goods became scarce. A thriving black market grew up around the Scotch Market in Rangoon in order to meet demand. Years later, when the economy was liberalized, the black market in consumer goods disappeared.

In 2008 Myanmar changed course. Article 35 of the 2008 Constitution makes clear that "the economic system of the Union is [the] market economy system". The world has been invited back in. Monopolies are prohibited. The country seeks to reassure foreign investors by providing assurances against expropriation. Under the new government, Myanmar has become strong enough to once again export rice. It is now the world's ninth largest rice exporter. Agriculture and fisheries play important roles in the country's economy.

Natural gas and gems are the country's largest exports. Since 1989, Myanmar has been a regular exporter of natural gas to Thailand. Natural gas is used to generate electricity and power automobiles in Thailand, Myanmar's second-largest trading partner. However, the Myanmar government has announced that in the future it will need much of its production for domestic needs.

Despite previous U.S. restrictions on the importation of Burmese rubies and jadeite, the gem export trade continues to be profitable and with the elimination of sanctions, even more so. Construction plays an increasingly important role in the economy, as does tourism. Tourism is only 1% of GDP but constitutes a growing sector. There is a new airport and more foreign airlines have acquired slots. The old airport's former VIP terminal was converted into a new terminal to help cope with the increasing numbers of airline passengers.

From 1998 to 2010 Myanmar's GDP tripled and reached 54 billion dollars. By 2015, according to the World Bank, GDP had grown to 64.8 billion. While this level of growth is extraordinary, to put this number in perspective compare Thailand, with a roughly similar population and a GDP of 319 billion. The Asian Development Bank expects Myanmar's economy to grow by at least 7-8% per year over the next several years, with a projection of 8.4Price, Waterhouse expects a more conservative 5.5%.

For the past twenty years there have generally been good relations and strong economic ties with both China and Thailand. Thai businesses have long been present in Myanmars economy. During the sanctions period, investing in Thai businesses that were active in Myanmar was one way to avoid any international violations. Thailand is a popular destination for overseas Burmese workers. There are approximately 3 million Burmese workers in Thailand. Of these, roughly half do not have proper immigration status in Thailand. Myanmar's workers in Thailand are a valuable source of remittances to their families in Myanmar.

Myanmar is a magnet for new foreign investment.

In August, 2016, Myanmar took in $731 million USD, primarily in the manufacturing sector. China is the largest foreign investor, ($14.1 bn) followed by Hong Kong ($6.4 bn), South Korea ($3.0 bn), Singapore ($2.4 bn), Malaysia ($1.6 bn) and Japan ($274 m).

Myanmar has bilateral investment treaties with China, India , Israel, Japan, , Korea, Kuwait, Laos, ,the Philippines, Thailand and Viet Nam. Myanmar, as a member of ASEAN (Association of Southeast Asian Nations), is a party to the ASEAN Comprehensive Investment Agreement.

Investments by American investors are growing. This is not surprising since formerly restrictive American sanctions made doing business in the Union a practical impossibility.

Still, the shadow of the past also darkens investors' views. Myanmar is held back by red tape and pervasive government controls. Myanmar once expropriated almost all foreign business. If the Army were to feel threatened due to their loss of power, would a general order "about face" and seize foreign assets? Probably not, but Turkey is an example of a country that once fully-embraced secularism only to turn back towards political Islam. The problem is that there are no guarantees and the risk of renewed expropriation is a real one, despite promises to the contrary.

Despite these shadows, the country's economic liberalization promises explosive growth and development over the next several years. As economic liberalization often accompanies political liberalization, the West can hardly complain.

CHAPTER 5

Legal System

The observer will find a visit to the Burmese courts a throwback to another era. Scribes sit at manual typewriters in front of the courthouse preparing pleadings on revenue stamped paper for litigants. Compared to the elaborate formality of trials at the Old Bailey, the Burmese courts can appear informal, but this is not really the case.

Myanmar's legal system is a unique combination of traditional law, codified English law, local case law and legislation. The common law has been the law of Burma, subject to local custom, since 1885. As a former British colony, Burma was once included amongst the family of common law nations. Within a short time after the country fell to English control, Burmese courts were patterned after the English system.

The Burma Code is composed of thirteen volumes of codified laws passed from 1841-1954. In addition to the Burma Courts Manual, there are numerous special laws, notifications, rules, regulations and orders. The

Government publishes an official gazette advising of the promulgation of new legislation and rules.[1]

Article 226 of the 1947 constitution provided that all laws passed prior to the date of independence, that is, January 4, 1948, were to continue in force unless specifically repealed. Similarly, Article 202(b) of the 1974 socialist constitution provided for the continued applicability of those laws already in force that had not been amended or repealed. The new 2008 constitution confirms the applicability of existing law going forward. The net effect of the three constitutions with respect to existing British and traditional legislation as of 1947 is that many older laws continue in force.

During the colonial period, matters relating to marriage, inheritance and religion were covered by local laws, sometimes called the Burmese Code or the *Damasat*. In ancient times these laws were written on palm leaves and were restricted to family, religious and private matters. Because of tradition and their antiquity, the Code came to influence Burmese legal matters generally. In 1775 the *Damasat* was revised and in 1847 the Code was first translated into English to be used in British-administered Burmese courts.

The *Damasat* is divided into ten volumes. It was a comprehensive Code which treated all subjects that could be heard by the courts and not merely those that it would be permitted to address following the

---

[1]*Doing Business in Myanmar*, Myanmar Legal Services Ltd., 9 September 2015

commencement of British rule. Early scholars found similarities with the ancient Indian Laws of Manu, compiled between 200 BC and 200 AD. According to tradition, the eighteen original laws given by Manu to the ruler are:

- Borrowing money.
- Deposits of money.
- Stealing and altering the appearance of property and selling it.
- When a gift may be had back on demanding it, and when not, there being six kinds of gifts.
- Deciding the wages of carpenters.
- Deciding the wages of laborers.
- Breach of promise.
- Deciding disputes between the owners of cattle and neat-herds.
- Settling disputed boundaries.
- Deciding whether property purchased may be returned.
- Accusations.
- Theft or concealment.
- Assault.
- Murder.
- Deciding the proper conduct of husband and wife.
- The question of slavery.
- Deciding if cock-fighting, betting, or gambling debts shall be paid.
- Partition of inherited property.

The *Phyathon* was a collection of decisions of the

pre-colonial royal court that were of little use upon the reception of the common law. During the colonial period, reported English and Indian decisions outlined the rule of law.

5.1   Contracts

Under the *Damasat* there were two kinds of promises. Only promises made in an unemotional state were binding. Those made under the influence of emotion, such as fear or anger, were considered non-binding. A binding promise, like an option in Anglo-American law, was considered the property of the obligee. Sales were conditional for a five-day period in order to mitigate the harshness of caveat emptor. In this way, the Burmese traditional doctrine stands somewhere between the Roman/Western system which ignores asymmetrical information to the Islamic system which prohibits any kind of uncertainty. If within five days a buyer finds that he has paid an exorbitant price the sale can be rescinded. Similarly, if a defect is discovered within that time period the sale can be rescinded. While these rules became obsolete with the reception of the common law, the fact that the *Damasat* continued—and continues—to be used in the realm of personal and religious matters means that its principles find their way into modern legal arguments.

Today, the Contract Act and common law contract analysis apply. Lawyers with a common law background will find themselves moored in a safe harbor of familiar legal language. There is no contract without offer and acceptance. A contract will fail for lack of consideration. A party must be competent to contract. The object of the contract must be legal.

Myanmar courts will honor a contract forum selection clause or a referral to arbitration. Foreign arbitration is permitted if not contrary to public policy. The jurisdiction of Myanmar courts cannot be waived entirely as such a provision is void under section 28 of the Contract Act. See chapter 6, *Arbitration*.

5.2   Witnesses

The *Damasat* disqualifies certain classes of witnesses as incompetent. These included the presiding judge, the parties and their families, friends and enemies. The sick, aged, children, women of ill repute, goldsmiths, blacksmiths, haters ("those who are inclined to harbor hatred"), gluttons, gamesters, thieves, physicians, those without a fixed place of abode, pregnant women and hermaphrodites. A witness who after testifying enters the home of a party is disqualified. Similarly, if a party visits the home of a witness before judgment is given he forfeits the case.

Some of these categories are enlightened: the testimony of either friends or enemies of a party can be expected to be biased. For judicial economy, their testimony is excluded. The incompetence of other witnesses is more difficult to understand. It is possible that rather than comprising a fixed list of classes the list is somewhat anecdotal. In the United States, all are deemed competent to testify, no matter how biased they may be. Under Islam, greater weight is given to the testimony of male Muslims above all other witnesses; in certain kinds of cases, the testimony of even one such worthy witness is insufficient. It is clear also that the traditional legal system took pains to avoid tampering or influencing witnesses by imposing severe consequences.

A party who refuses the testimony of a competent witness forfeits his case; the same is true if he fails to produce witnesses or these witnesses fail to take the oath. A party who takes an oath and testifies, however, need not present other witnesses.

5.3   Other Laws

As a province of British India, the Indian Statutes were applicable. These codes were based on the common law and English legislation, and included the Arbitration Act, the Companies Act, the Contract Act, the

Negotiable Instruments Act, the Registration Act, the Sale of Goods Act, the Transfer of Property Act, the Trusts Act and the Codes of Criminal and Civil Procedure. Recent decisions confirm that pre-1962 case law will be followed in the future.

During the past five years, at least 75 new laws have been enacted in such areas as employment, foreign investment, foreign exchange, securities regulation and government structure. So many new laws means that until procedures are established and agreed on, there will be ambiguity. Having different and overlapping foundations for government procedures in addition to the law itself can also be a contemporary source of uncertainty.

5.4   Judicial Administration

The Supreme Court is the highest court of Myanmar. However, its jurisdiction does not extend to courts-martial or matters within the jurisdiction of the constitutional court, called the Constitutional Tribunal of the Union. Below the Supreme Court are fourteen State or Divisional courts. Under these, there are 63 district courts. There are 323 courts of first instance or general jurisdiction called Township Courts. There are also inferior special courts that handle matter such as juvenile, municipal and traffic offenses. There is also a separate military court system.

Historically, the judge was paid 10% of the matter at issue as a fee to decide a case. Many matters were settled informally before local chieftains. The penultimate Burmese King, King Mindon, introduced the concept of fixed salaries for formal judicial officers, so by the time the British took control of Burma the practice of paying judges salaries irrespective of the amount of the cases before them was not an innovation.

The Union Supreme Court's Action Plan for 2013-2014 pledges support for the rule of law and promises to upgrade the integrity of the court system. A training program is planned for sitting judges and court infrastructure improvements will be made. Housing is also promised for judges and court officers. There is no jury system in Myanmar. Cases are tried before a single judge. The official language is Burmese. Foreign language documents must be translated in order to be admissible. Rules of proceedings are based on British colonial court rules and should be familiar to any Anglo-American lawyer. They are governed by the Civil Procedure Code, the Criminal Procedure Code and the Courts manual, all of which are available in Myanmar and English. Reported decisions of the Supreme Court are published in the Burma/Myanmar Law Reports. These decisions have precedential value.

5.5 Torts

In general, English common law principles and reasoning apply. There is joint and several liability as well as vicarious liability. There is no mandatory joinder rule requiring that all tortfeasors be made a party to the action. The term used for an initial pleading is "plaint", not "complaint". A plaint must state a cause of action and be written on stamped paper. After filing, it must be served on the defendant. A summons must be signed by a judge or the clerk of court. Plaints are sealed prior to service. Service may be personal or on an agent. Service against a company is effective if made at the company's registered Myanmar office or any place of business in Myanmar. If the company has no Myanmar registered office, service on the company's manager in Myanmar is effective. Lawyers may also accept service on behalf of their clients. If a defendant is avoiding service, substitute service is available, either by public posting or any other method the court deems reasonable. If there is no way to make service within Myanmar, registered mail may be used to effect service abroad. Before a defendant has answered, the plaintiff may take a voluntary dismissal. Afterwards, leave of court is required to dismiss an action.

A Myanmar court may stay proceedings where the parties have an arbitration agreement in place.

5.6   Discovery

"Discovery" is the technical term for a process by which parties litigant exchange relevant information and even information which might lead to relevant information prior to trial. Discovery is permitted, though this is not as expansive as one might find in the United States or the United Kingdom.

5.7   Trial

Except for arbitrations, the Evidence Act of 1872 applies.

5.8   Judgment

Common law remedies are available, including damages and both temporary and permanent injunctions. Damages are extremely conservative. Neither punitive damages or damages multipliers, such as treble damages in antitrust cases in some countries, applies.

Final foreign judgments may be enforced. As is the case with most countries, attempting to enforce a foreign judgment usually requires some relitigation of the facts if only to prove what happened in another court. For this reason, the effort is always duplicative, expensive, and should be avoided at all costs. It is always difficult to ask the courts of a foreign country to analyze the laws of another, especially when even local lawyers can so rarely agree on even the most simple principles.

The English rule on costs applies; that is, it is customary for a prevailing party to be awarded the costs of the action, including attorneys fees.

Lawyers

The existence of lawyers predates the colonial period. Not all the petitioners who made requests of the King could speak Burmese. Translators assisted them. Out of these humble origins the legal profession grew. The King acted as judge and those who stood before him on behalf of the parties were called *Shay-nay*.[2]

In colonial Burma there were two types of lawyers: the "Higher Grade Pleader" and the "Advocate". A "Higher Grade Pleader" in Burma is a legal practitioner admitted to practice in all Burmese courts except the Supreme Court. The Advocate is admitted to

---

[2] See, Scott, James George, Sir, *The Burman, His Life and Notions* (London) 1882

all Burmese courts. One must first be qualified as a Higher Grade Pleader before becoming an Advocate. A law graduate must complete a one-year internship with an Advocate in order to qualify. After working as a Higher Grade Pleader for one year, the lawyer can apply for admission as an Advocate. The distinction continues today. As of June 2005 there were 7000 Advocates and roughly 30,000 Higher Grade Pleaders.

Lawyers who had at least five years experience in another British jurisdiction were entitled to admission on motion. Others were subject to a bar examination and were tested on the laws of evidence, criminal and civil procedure and the penal code.

Up until the time of the socialist government, education in Burmese universities was conducted primarily in English. This was especially the case for legal education since so much of the primary materials were written in English. The socialist government then changed the language of instruction to Burmese and the courts followed suit. By 1970, all reports of decisions were written in the Burmese language only. After 1988, when the government slowly opened up to reforms, English was reinstated as the language of instruction for legal education. Nevertheless, Article 102 of the 2008 Constitution provides that "[t]he Burmese language shall be used in the administration of justice."

Even though legal education is now once again provided in English, the reports of decisions continue to be written solely in Burmese. It is of course, unreasonable to expect that a judge who has written opinions throughout his career in one language will instantaneously switch to another because of the country's about-face with respect to language policy. It remains to be seen, as Burmese lawyers return to English, whether English will break out of the confines of the academy so as to be used once again in the law reports. There is a precedent for this, as the Malaysian courts, another former British colony, issue decisions both in English as well as in Malaysian. Certainly the lack of reported decisions in English after 1970 complicates legal research for non-Burmese practitioners.

5.9 Arbitration

Myanmar joined the New York Convention on the Recognition and Enforcement of Foreign Arbitration Awards effective 15 July 2013. Myanmar enacted the Arbitration Law on 5 January 2016 (Pyidaungsu Hluttaw Law No. 5/2016) repealing the Arbitration Act of 1944 as well as older arbitration rules date from 1861. The simplicity of the 1861 Rules is worth examining, if for no other reason than to show how rules become bloated over time.

> 1. Both the parties shall have notice of the time and place of meeting of the arbitrators, and both

the parties shall have a right to be present, either in person or by a pleader, or authorized agent at every sitting of the arbitrators. If either of the parties fail to appear after due notice, the arbitrators may proceed in the manner directed in the Code for default of parties.

2. The arbitrators shall make notes of their proceedings at each sitting with a summary of the examination of the parties and the depositions of the witnesses.

3. These notes may be written in any language the arbitrators please. They need not be translated, unless either of the parties move to set aside the award, or to reduce the fees charged by the arbitrators, in which case if the notes are in any other language than English or Burmese, and the Court requires to refer to them, it will order them to be translated into one or other of those languages, at the cost, in the first instance, of the party objecting, and chargeable afterwards as costs of suit.

4. The arbitrators may examine the parties or their witnesses, with or without oath, as they deem fit, and are authorized to administer oaths accordingly.

5. If the arbitrators reject any documentary evidence tendered by either party, or refuse to examine any witness, named by either party, they shall note that fact, and the reason of such rejection or refusal, upon their proceedings.

6. The mode of conducting an arbitration, subject to the above general rules, is left to the arbitrators. [3]

---

[3] *Rules for the Better Regulation of Cases referred to Arbitration*, 18 July 1861.

Paragraph 7 of the Arbitration Law establishes the basic principle of judicial non-interference with arbitrations. Judicial involvement shall be the exception rather than the rule. The law applies to both domestic and international disputes. There is no bar preventing domestic parties from selecting international arbitration as a method of dispute resolution. Objections to arbitration must be made "without undue delay.'otherwise the grounds are waived. The objections are for the most part jurisdictional:

(1) Arbitral tribunal has no jurisdiction;

(2) Procedural defect in arbitration process;

(3) Failure to comply with the arbitration agreement or provisions of this Law;

(4) Detrimental impact on the arbitral tribunal or arbitration due to procedural defect.

¶6.

The arbitral agreement must be in writing and signed by the parties. ¶9(a)(2). classifies electronic communications as meeting the "writing'requirement, but is silent as to how such a "writing'may be signed. Lawsuits shall be stayed where the parties are referred to arbitration. ¶10. Importantly, domestic courts retain significant interim injunctive powers during the pendency of an arbitration. Among these are:

(1) taking evidence;

(2) the preservation of any evidence;

(3) pass an order related to the property in disputes in arbitration or any property which is related to the subject-matter of the dispute;

(4) inspection, taking photo for evidence, preservation and seizure of the property which is related to the dispute;

(5) samples to be taken from, or any observation to be made of or experiment conducted upon, any property which is or forms part of the subject-matter of the dispute;

(6) allow to enter in the premises owned by or under the control of the parties to disputes for the purpose of above mentions matters;

(7) sale of any property which is the subject-matter of the dispute;

(8) an interim injunction or appointment of a receiver;

Unless the parties agree otherwise, a sole arbitrator will decide the arbitration. An individual of any nationality may act as arbitrator. If a party fails to nominate his own arbitrator according to his agreement or fails to cooperate in the arbitration, the counterparty may ask the Chief Justice of the Union in an international arbitration or the agreed arbitration institution to nominate an arbitrator on his behalf. An arbitrator must be both impartial and possess the predetermined qualifications specified by the parties. The lack of either disqualifies the arbitrator. Even though the parties may have selected a particular city as the seat of arbitration, the tribunal itself may decide to meet in any place it considers convenient for deliberations or for the taking of evidence. ¶23. The proceedings may be conducted in any language. ¶25. Unless the parties agree, it will be up to the arbitral tribunal to decide if hearings need to be held. However, unless the parties have agreed that no hearings shall be held, the arbitral tribunal shall hold such hearings at an appropriate stage of the proceedings, if so requested by a party. ¶27(a). The arbitral tribunal may request judicial assistance for the purpose of obtaining evidence. ¶30. In domestic arbitrations, the substantive law of Myanmar shall apply. ¶32(a). In international arbitrations, the parties may select the substantive law to apply. ¶32(b). Even two domestic parties may select the law of a jurisdiction other than Myanmar and a seat of arbitration outside the Union for what would otherwise be a wholly domestic affair. The award made by the arbitral tribunal is final and binding. ¶38. Article 46 contains rules for the enforcement of foreign arbitral awards. In general, arbitral awards are given the same force and effect as domestic court judgments. Enforcement will be refused where:

(1) the parties to the arbitration agreement referred was under some incapacity; or

(2) the said agreement is not valid under the law to which the parties have subjected to it or, failing any indication thereon, under the law of the country where the award was made;

(3) the party against whom the award is invoked was not given proper notice of the appointment of an arbitrator or of the arbitral proceedings or was otherwise unable to present his case; or

(4) the award deals with a dispute not contemplated by or not falling within the terms of the submission to arbitration, or it contains decisions on matters beyond the scope of the submission to arbitration; or

(5) the composition of the arbitral tribunal or the arbitral procedure was not in accordance with the agreement of the parties or, failing such agreement, was not in accordance with the law of the country where the arbitration took place; or

(6) the award has not yet become binding on the parties or has been set aside or suspended by a competent authority of the country in which, or under the law of which, that award was made.

There is a public policy exception to enforcement as well as an exception where the subject matter of the arbitration would not be capable of resolution under Myanmar law, such as criminal matters and bankruptcy. During the pendency of the arbitration, Myanmar courts have jurisdiction to enforce the interim orders of the foreign arbitral tribunal. Otherwise, the Myanmar courts will not intervene absent specific authority. Myanmar courts have the obligation of referring the parties to arbitration where they have chosen arbitration as their method of resolving disputes. An exception exists where the underlying contract is a nullity. ¶¶7,10. Appeals may be taken where a court has ordered or refused to order a party to arbitration or where a court has refused to enforce a foreign award. ¶47(a).

CHAPTER 6

Foreign Trade

Myanmar has a long history of trading with the outside world. Trade was conducted with China even before that nation was opened up by Western traders.

Trade was on the basis of barter rather than buying and selling. Rice was bartered for fish and other foodstuffs. Rangoon's port attracted merchants from all parts of India and Arabia. Because there were easily accessible forests of teak in Burma, teak prices and availability were much lower than in other places in the Empire. Teak, a light colored heavy wood, was sought after because of its well-known natural flotation properties. There were stories of ships carrying teak cargoes that had become swamped with water yet did not sink. Teak was a prized export, and Burmese teak was considered to be of a very high quality.

After 1962, businesses that were engaged in foreign trade were for the most part nationalized. Obtaining foreign exchange to pay for foreign goods became impossible except for government enterprises. The little foreign trade that did occur was with Myanmar's historic regional trading partners, China and Thailand. In the absence of official permission, black market and unregulated cross-border trade thrived.

Foreign investment in 2014 reached $8 billion USD for the year, but dropped to $3.9 billion USD for 2015. That figure grew to $9.4 billion for the fiscal year ending March, 2016. McKinsey Global estimates that foreign direct investment may reach as much as $100 billion by 2030.

Today, Myanmar's economy is diverse and offers many opportunities. Agriculture is of great significance to the economy because it contributes from 43-60% of the country's GDP (estimates vary). 70% of the country's jobs are tied to agriculture.

The Union government seeks foreign investment, on either a 100% foreign owned or joint venture basis for the establishment of agricultural industries, for manufacturing light agricultural machinery and farm implements and other agricultural support products. Crops such as cotton, jute, rubber, vegetable oils, palm, cashews and fruits such as mangoes, bananas and watermelon are specific targets. The Ministry of Agriculture operates eight sugar mills on a joint venture basis. The Maximum Sustainable Yield for fisheries is estimated at 1.05 million metric tons annually.

Myanmar offers mining opportunities with respect to granite and limestone and remains one of the world's primary sources of top-quality ornamental stones.

The government also seeks BOT (Build, Operate

and Transfer) and joint venture partners for the construction of roads, inland cargo depots and ports. Similarly, in the power generation sector, foreign direct investment is focused on hydropower and can be accomplished on a BOT and joint venture basis. Local investors are also permitted to invest in Independent Power Producer hydropower projects.

CHAPTER 7

New Foreign Investment Law

Myanmar's new foreign investment law has been planned since 2013. The new law, was endorsed by the country's legislative bodies on October 18, 2016 to take effect on April 1, 2017. The new law combines the Foreign Investment Law of 2013 and the Citizens' Investment Law.

The draft Foreign Investment Law repeals and replaces both the Foreign Investment Law (2012 Pyidaungsu Hluttaw Law. No. 21) and the Myanmar Citizens Investment Law (2013 Phidaungsu Hluttaw Law No. 18). The new law defines "Foreign Investor"as any investor who is not a citizen. This includes foreign companies, branch offices and other entities established under the Myanmar Companies Act as well as business entities formed under the laws of foreign countries. In order to invest in the Union, a foreign investor must establish a company, partnership or sole proprietorship.

The law applies to all current and future investments in Myanmar. It does not apply to any pending investment disputes.

Interestingly, health, safety and national security exemptions previously imposed will not be applicable to the law. It is not clear what this will mean in practice, since Chapters 21 and 22 of the law contain broad language which grants discretion to the government to prohibit investments or activities for these reasons.

The law is administered by the Myanmar Investment Commission ("MIC"). The Commission is the main government agency tasked with coordinating and monitoring all foreign investment in the Union. As such, the Commission has both strategic as well as a regulatory responsibilities. The Commission is composed of nine members whose terms of office will be coterminous with the government. The Secretary is responsible for the Commission's day-to-day operations. The Secretary of the Commission is deemed a civil servant subject to the Civil Service Law. Members may serve only two consecutive terms. To avoid conflicts of interest, Commission members must report any interest in a matter before the Commission. They are similarly prohibited from taking personal advantage from information gleaned during their tenure with the Commission. The Commission coordinates tax exemptions granted for specific foreign investments along with other government agencies. Business proposals covering strategic and infrastructure investments must be submitted to the Commission. The Commission will study each proposal and issue an investment permit after appropriate review. To facilitate communication with foreign investors, the MIC moved from the capital Nay Pyi Taw to Yangon in 2014.

Strategic and capital intensive investments required the submission of a business proposal to the Commission.

7.0.1 Permitted Business

Investments may concern:

a. Organization of new business;

b. Moveable property, immovable property and related property rights, cash, pledges, mortgages and liens, machinery, equipment, spare-parts, and related tools;

c. shares, stocks, and debentures of a company;

d. intellectual property, including technical know-how, inventions, industrial designs, and trademarks;

e. claims to money and to any performance under contract having a financial value;

f. rights under contracts, including turnkey, construction, management, production or revenue- sharing contracts; and

g. assignable rights granted by relevant laws or contract including the rights of exploration and extraction of natural resources;

7.0.2   Prohibited List

The following businesses are excluded from the foreign investment regime:

a. importation of hazardous or poisonous waste;

b. importation of unproven technologies, medicines or instruments or which have not obtained relevant approvals for use, planting or cultivation;

c. businesses which may adversely affect traditional culture and customs of the racial groups within the Union;

d. businesses which may affect public health;

e. businesses which may cause damage to the natural environment and ecosystem; and

f. manufacture of prohibited goods.

Also see discussion in Chapter Ten, *Commencing Business*, "Negative List."

7.0.3   Restricted Areas

Several areas are not prohibited, but restricted:

a. Sectors where only the Union Government is allowed to undertake and where both domestic and foreign investments are prohibited;

b. Sectors where only foreign investment is prohibited;

c. Sectors where foreign investment is allowed only in joint ventures with a citizen-owned entity or with a citizen of Myanmar; and

d. Sectors where both domestic and foreign investment require approval from relevant ministries.

The Commission is tasked with notifying the Union government of any investment which may have a significant effect on security or economic conditions, the environment or the health, safety and welfare of the country. Presumably, the Union government will step in and prevent the issuance of investment licenses in light of policy questions raised by any such notification.

7.0.4   Employment

The new Foreign Investment Law permits the appointment of a foreign national to manage operations. Training programs are required for Myanmar nationals and unskilled labor is restricted to Myanmar nationals. At a minimum, employment contracts entered into under a Foreign Investment Permit must meet those minimums stipulated in existing labor laws and regulations. If a foreign investor sponsors foreign nationals to work in the Union, he is responsible for their conduct. As a consequence, if the misbehavior of an employee is serious enough, it could jeopardize the foreign investment permit itself. Since the Commission imposes progressive penalties, not all employee misbehavior threatens existing foreign investment permits.

A business may cease operations only upon payment of dues owed to employees.

7.0.5   Expropriation

The government has pledged non-expropriation guarantees for businesses properly licensed under the Foreign Investment Law. This is a substantial commitment, especially given that almost all foreign businesses were expropriated in 1962. Expropriation of foreign investment is subject to the payment of fair and adequate compensation in accordance with the rule of law. The value of the property shall be its market value at the time of expropriation. Indirect takings are also recognized and subject to the expropriation provisions of the law.

7.0.6   Transfer of Funds

There are no restrictions on the repatriation or the transfer of funds outside of Myanmar except with respect to capital account rules on capital issued by the Central Bank of Myanmar. Transfers on incoming funds which are subject to taxes may only be made upon a showing that taxes have been paid. The Union government is required to permit the transfer of capital from abroad for the project. However, in case of serious balance-of-payments issues or a financial crisis, the government may impose restrictions on transfers in accordance with the Foreign Exchange Management Law of 2012. In practice, what this means is that the free transfer of funds will be permitted until prohibited. Foreign investors must therefore be pro-active in monitoring business trends including currency fluctuations.

7.0.7   Customs Duties

General tax holidays are no longer automatically granted to new foreign business. Tax exemptions can include customs duty on imported products and raw materials. An income tax exemption is permitted where profits are re-invested in the business within one year, subject to Commission approval. Because the Foreign Investment Law applies to all businesses currently in operation as well as prospectively, applications for tax exemptions may be entertained under Chapter 19 even though no application or exemption has been previously granted. There is no special tax rate for foreign business; taxes will be imposed in a non-discriminatory fashion on foreign and national enterprises alike. Businesses operating in Special Economic Zones are subject to different tax rules. If a business receives a tax exemption which it uses to import materiel and machinery for a project that is discontinued, the foreign investor can export the machinery, pay the customs duty owed or apply for relief. Tax relief generally will be granted on a case by case basis where the investment promotes the country's development in specified regions or sectors. Tax relief is not automatic and must be applied for.

7.0.8   Regulations

Implementing regulations in effect before the passage of the law remain in effect pending issuance of new regulations. However, if the former regulations contradict the new law, the new law shall take precedence. Previously existing permits remain in effect.

7.0.9   Duty to Submit Proposals

"Strategic"businesses involving capital-intensive projects or which potentially could have serious environmental impact, as well as specific businesses designated by the government, must obtain permission from the Commission before a foreign investment license can be granted. This permission is obtained after a detailed proposal is submitted to the Commission, containing all the necessary permits required. This means that licenses must be obtained prior to obtaining the Commission's approval for a project, a potentially perilous problem since obtaining necessary environmental permits is often a lengthy process and there is no guarantee that the Commission will approve a project even though other ministries issue licenses in anticipation of the Commission's approval.

Where a foreign investment involves the use or exploitation of land, a proposal must also be submitted to the Commission for endorsement. In this case as well, all the necessary licenses must be issued and attached to the proposal.

7.0.10   Treatment of Investors

Foreign investors are to be accorded no less favorable treatment than Myanmar citizens with respect to the "expansion, management, operation, and the sale or other disposition of direct investments."The law also requires that all foreign investors be treated alike, i.e., that nationals of one country are not given preference over nationals of another, except with respect to any Customs Union, Free Trade Zone, Economic Union or pursuant to treaty. Thus, ASEAN nationals may be accorded preferential treatment. Under the new law, the Union government commits itself to guarantee fair and equitable treatment of foreign investors and their investments.

7.0.11   Real Estate, Land Use

Before the passage of the new Foreign Investment Law, foreign companies were prohibited from acquiring land for a period in excess of one year without special per-

mission from the government. Now, foreign investors
have the right to obtain a long-term lease of land either
from private land-holders or from the government in
the case of state-owned land. The term of these leases
is fifty years commencing on the date of the granting of
a foreign investment license by the Commission. The
Commission may approve two ten year extensions, for
a total period of seventy years. Leases are to be registered at the Registrar Office of Deeds and Assurances.
For land leases in remote or economically disadvan-
taged areas, the Commission has the authority to grant
a longer lease term.

7.0.12   Responsibilities of Investors

Investors must establish or register a company or part-
nership under Union law in order to do business in
Myanmar. Those who wish to do business in Myanmar
must also:
- Obey local laws, including tax laws
- Obtain all required licenses, permits and permis-
  sions
- Report the discovery of natural resources or trea-
  sure
- Preserve natural topography
- Keep proper books and records
- Pay employees their dues
- Pay workers compensation in case of injury or
  accident

- Enjoy the right to sue and be sued
- Pay compensation in case of unlicensed natural resource extraction
- Carry appropriate insurance.

7.0.13 Dispute Resolution

The law requires the Commission to set up a dispute resolution system to manage claims. Disputes shall be settled in either the Union's courts or through arbitration. Presumably a investment license may require arbitration under the Commission's dispute resolution mechanism.

7.0.14 Penalties

An investor who violates the Foreign Investment Law may be subject to penalties including,
- Censure
- Suspension of tax exemption or benefits
- Revocation of the license
- Blacklisting the company

The investor may contest the imposition of any such penalty.

7.0.15 Exemptions

There are general health and welfare, law enforcement and national security exemptions under which the Union government may step in and take non-discriminatory action for "prudent reasons."

7.1   Special Economic Zones

A new Myanmar Special Economic Zone Law was enacted in 2014. This law repealed the former Special Economic Zone and the Dawei Special Economic Zone Law. Businesses located in these areas have greater privileges than those licensed under the Foreign Investment Law. The General Body for the Myanmar Special Economic Zones was formed in April 2011 to regulate the Zones. Among the benefits are:

- Five-year tax holiday
- Five-year 50% income tax reduction on profits from sale of exported products
- Five-year 50% income tax reduction on reinvestment based on revenue from export sales
- Five-year 100% customs duty exemption for machinery and vehicles, 50% reduction for the following five years
- no customs duty within the free zones
- 100% foreign ownership (this is a separate concession from that conferred by the new FIL);
- 50 year land lease with a 25 year renewable period;
- 5 year income tax exemption for investment business in the Promotion Zones or other businesses in the boundary of the SEZ
- 50% income tax reduction for investment business–first five years
- 50% income tax reduction–third five years if reinvested within one year in the business as a reserve fund;

- Reimbursement of customs duties on raw materials and goods used for production if used in the SEZ;
- five year loss carry-forward;
- addition exemptions (VAT and commercial tax) for manufactured and exported goods
- exported goods entitled to exemption of taxes and other assessments;
- exemption of tax on dividends for SEZ profits;
- Right to open foreign currency accounts with approved banks;
- Non-expropriation guarantee during the permitted period.

Special Economic Zones have been set up for the following activities:

Production Based:

- Goods processing
- High-tech products manufacturing
- Light manufacturing
- Agriculture-based industries
- Livestock breeding and fisheries
- Mineral produce based industries
- Forestry produce based industries

Services Based:

- Trading
- Logistics and transportation
- Storage and warehousing
- Hotel and tourism
- Education and health

- Residential housing
- Infrastructure, supply and support centers
- Green areas
- Recreation and resort industries

In the Special Economic Zones, new businesses must "bear the expenses of transferring and paying compensation of houses, buildings, farms and gardens, orchards, fields,

and

plantation on land."This condition can quickly mire a foreign investor in local disputes. Former landowners in the Dawei SEZ claim that they have not been fairly compensated. The issue of land titles is one that calls for not only due diligence but extreme caution. There currently are five Special Economic Zones: Thilawa (Yangon), Kyank Phyu(Rakhine State), Dawei (Tanintharyi Division), Kokang (Shan State) and Myawaddy (Karen State) SEZ. Of the five SEZ's, Dawei, Thilawa and Kyank Phyu have commenced operations. The Dawei SEZ, unlike the others, permits trading.

CHAPTER 8

Myanmar Companies Law 2015

The new Myanmar companies law, styled the Myanmar Companies Law 2015, was planned for passage in 2015 but it has not yet been approved. The law replaces former legislation including the Indiana Companies Act 1866 and 1882 and the Burma Companies Act 1914. The Special Company Act 1950 is also repealed. ¶414. [1]The law also repeals sections of the Myanmar Companies Rules 1940 ¶409(1) and the Myanmar Companies Regulations 1957.

The law defines "foreign company"as a company owned or controlled by non-Myanmar interests. The precise ownership percentage is not stated in the law, but the terms "owns or controls"are well understood. The Directorate of Investment and Company Administration is tasked with registering and regulating both existing and new companies under the law. ¶361. The Directorate performs the duties of Registrar. No special

---

[1]References are to paragraphs in the new draft law.

courts were created under the law to handle company-related disputes. Instead the regular courts of Myanmar have jurisdiction. Under the law, companies are either public or private. ¶4. Private companies may have no more than fifty shareholders. There is no similar limit on public companies. Foreign companies ¶5(b) and "business associations"may also register under the law. Holding companies may register. ¶4(2). Companies formed under the Special Companies Act 1950 or any previous law must re-register as companies limited by shares. ¶37(2). Foreign corporations are not affected. ¶37(3). If necessary, a re-registration may require modification of a company's name if the current name lacks identifying terms concerning liability. ¶38. An association or partnership may consist of no more than ten members for engaging in banking business. ¶40(a). For-profit partnerships are limited to twenty persons. ¶40(b). This could affect many service businesses, especially law, consulting and accounting firms. Family businesses are excluded. The penalties for violation of this provision are extreme and entail a loss of limited liability.

Non-profit organizations are recognized and should be registered as corporations. ¶41(1). A non-profit company may keep the identities of its members private.

Companies may be formed by a sole member/shareholder. (¶6). At least one company director must be ordinarily resident in Myanmar. ¶6(e). This provision has generated some controversy as it is unpopular with the foreign business community. If the provision is kept in the final version of the law, it will create an opportunity for company formation entities to provide nominee local resident directors as a component of their company formation services.

A company may engage in any legal business. ¶7(1)(b). This is an innovation as previously a company was restricted to that business identified in the company's constitution or articles of association. Amending these was a time-consuming task.

A company is either a limited or unlimited liability company. Shareholders may either limit their liability to their shareholdings or a guarantee in a stated amount.

Paragraph 8 of the law sets forth in detail the information required for registration of a company. Paragraph 9 prohibits the Registrar from requiring additional documents. In theory, registration should be automatic and a certificate of incorporation issued upon the presentation of only those documents mentioned in the law, unless the Minister has required additional documents. Thus, what one section grants–automatic registration–another takes away: "[except those] as may be prescribed by the Minister."

A company is required to have a constitutive document, known as its constitution, in other countries this document is often referred to as a company's articles of association. The constitution may grant powers in addition to those specified in the law to the company's board. The constitution must specify that the company's registered office will be located in Myanmar.

A company with limited liability shall carry the word "Limited"or the abbreviation "Ltd."as the last word in its name. ¶14a. The constitution shall state the liability of its shareholders is limited; shall identify the classes of shares to be issued and the currency denomination of such shares. A shareholder must own at least one share. Improper use of the word "limited"is prohibited and subject to a fine. ¶395.

A company limited by guarantee shall include the term, "Limited by Guarantee"or "Ltd Gty"as the last word in its name. ¶15. The constitution must state that the liability of the members is limited by the amount of the guarantee. In the case of winding up the company, the members will contribute up to a specified amount. The guarantee company shall identify the classes of shares to be issued and the currency denomination of such shares. A shareholder must own at least one share. ¶15.

Similarly, a company without limited liability shall include the term "Unlimited"as the last word in its name. The constitution must state that the liability of its members is unlimited and the company shall identify the classes of shares to be issued and the currency denomination of such shares. A shareholder must own at least one share. ¶16.

The constitution must be prepared in the Myanmar

language and have consecutive numbered paragraphs. ¶17. Bilingual versions are permitted.

The selection of a name for the new company is not a trivial matter. Companies must have new names that are not confusingly similar to the names of existing companies. ¶24. Companies may not use the word "bank"in their names or use any other name which suggests that the company is an official state entity. ¶24(3). The company must use its name in every written communication "sent by, or on behalf of the company."¶26(a), ¶117. Presumably, this includes emails.

The law sets forth rules for the execution of contracts and documents, with or without seal. ¶28. The law recognizes the doctrine of "apparent authority"in dealing with a properly-registered company. ¶¶29,30. Non-profit (business or economic development) companies may also be established. ¶41. It is unclear whether non-business development non-profits may also be established.

8.1 Foreign Companies

In order to do business in Myanmar, a foreign company must register under the Myanmar Companies Law. ¶42.

"Doing business"does not include those situations where an individual or a company:

- acts as a party to a legal proceeding or settles a legal proceeding or a claim or dispute;
- holds meetings of its directors or shareholders or carries on other activities concerning its internal affairs;
- maintains a bank account;
- effects a sale of property through an independent contractor;
- solicits or procures an order that becomes a binding contract only if the order is accepted outside the Republic of the Union of Myanmar;
- loans money, creates evidence of a debt or creates a charge on property;
- secures or collects any of its debts or enforces its rights in relation to securities relating to those debts;
- conducts an isolated transaction that is completed within a period of 30 days, not being one of a number of similar transactions repeated from time to time; or
- invests its funds or holds property. ¶42.

A company that wishes to register under the law must submit the following:

- the name of the overseas corporation;
- the full names, date of birth, gender, nationality and residential addresses of the directors and any secretary of the overseas corporation as of the date of the application;
- confirmation that the overseas corporation has

appointed an authorized officer, and provide the full name, date of birth and residential address of the authorized officer appointed by the overseas corporation (who will be authorized to accept service of documents in the Republic of the Union of Myanmar of documents on behalf of the overseas corporation);

- confirmation that the person named as the authorized officer has given their written consent to act as authorized officer the overseas corporation;
- the full address of the place of business in the Republic of the Union of Myanmar of the overseas corporation or, if the overseas corporation has more than one place of business in the Republic of the Union of Myanmar, the full address of the principal place of business in the Republic of the Union of Myanmar of the overseas corporation;
- the full address of its registered office or principal place of business in its place of origin;
- a declaration by the overseas corporation that all matters stated in the application are true and correct; and
- attach evidence of incorporation of the overseas corporation and a copy of the instrument constituting or defining the constitution of the corporation, and, if not in Myanmar language, a Myanmar language translation of such documents and a summary statement in the English language, duly certified by a company director.

¶45.

Changes in the foreign company's constitution, the composition of its board, a change of registered address or principal place of business or a change of its authorized officer must be submitted within 28 days of the effective date. ¶48. Annual reporting is required of foreign corporations and Paragraph 49 sets forth the contents of the annual report. Financial reports of the company's business activities in Myanmar must in any event be filed. ¶49(2).

Service of process on a foreign company registered under the law is through personal service at the company's registered address or at the registered address of its authorized officer. Service may also be effected by mail. ¶51.

Companies that have appointed managing agents to handle their business affairs in Myanmar must terminate these relationships and structure their business in accordance with the new MCL. ¶415.

8.2   Change in Status

A company may change from one type to another by passing a resolution to do so and filing an application with the Directorate. ¶52. Any change does not create a new legal entity or affect the company's existing rights or obligations. ¶54(1)(b).

Changing a guarantee company to a company limited by shares has the effect of extinguishing the members' liability as guarantor. ¶54(2).

8.3   Share Capital

Shares do not have a nominal or par value but the value assigned by the company's constitution. ¶55. Shareholders have equal voting and dividend rights. However, the company may issue different classes of shares which have preferential or restricted rights, or which do not have voting rights. *See*, ¶57.

Companies may issue debt and convertible securities. ¶57(2). A company may also create and grant mortgages. ¶195.

Shares may be issued at any time in accordance with the company's constitution. ¶58. For this reason plenary powers should be given to a company's board of directors in case business exigencies require the issuance of debt without having to amend the company's constitution.

New shares may be fully or partially paid. ¶58(2). Existing shareholders have preemptive rights. ¶58(3). A board will be taken to task if it accepts worthless consideration for shares. ¶59(2).

An issuance of shares that increases a member's liability is void without written consent. ¶62.

The company must report the issuances of new shares or securities to the Directorate within 21 days. ¶65.

The law presumes that records of share transfers will be maintained by companies on their own books. There appear to be no provisions for independent transfer agents. Nevertheless, all trades must be reported to the Directorate and rules for the transfer of the shares of publicly traded companies will be created as the Yangon Stock Exchange matures.

8.4   Members, Registers

Strangely, the law focuses on the term "member"rather than "shareholder"or "partner"to describe the participants in a business enterprise. It is not clear why this nomenclature was chosen. A company must keep a register of its members and report changes to the directorate. ¶¶79,80.

Registers of option holders and debt holders must also be kept. ¶¶81-83.

8.5   Annual Reports

Companies must file annual reports containing the following information:

(a) the registered name of the company;

(b) the registration number of the company;

(c) the address of the registered office of the company and, if different, the address of the place where the register of members is kept;

(d) in the case of a public company, a list of the 50 members (or such other number of members if the company has less than 50 members) holding the largest number of shares in the company and their respective names, addresses and nationalities and shareholdings;

(e) in any other case, a list of all members of the company and their respective names, addresses and nationalities and shareholdings and a list of persons who ceased to be members since the date of the last filing;

(f) the date of the last annual general meeting of the company (if applicable);

(g) particulars of the company's principal activity or activities at the date to which the accounts of the company are made up and at the date of the annual return;

(h) a summary distinguishing between shares issued for cash and shares issued as fully or partly paid up otherwise than in cash;

(i) the amount of the share capital of the company, and the number of the shares into which it is divided;

(j) the amount called up on each share;

(k) the total number of shares forfeited or cancelled since the date of the last return;

(l) whether the company is a foreign company;

(m) the names of the companys subsidiaries, holding companies and ultimate holding company, if any;

(n) the names, addresses, gender and nationality of the persons who at the date of the return are the directors of the company and of the persons (if any) who at the said date are the secretaries of the company, and the changes in the personnel of the directors and secretaries since the last return together with the dates on which they took place;

(o) confirmation that the mortgages and charges which are required to be registered with the Registrar under this Law have been registered; and

(p) such other items as may be prescribed from time to time.

¶86.

The courts of Myanmar are empowered to correct erroneous company registers. ¶89. Myanmar courts are also granted enforcement powers in cases of deadlock and have a role to play in company liquidations as well.

It is noteworthy that the Directorate does not set up any special administrative committees to rapidly adjudicate company matters rather than send litigants to the ordinary courts. On the other hand, the law recognizes that parties may use arbitration to resolve their disputes. Arbitration is not mandatory.

8.6 Dividends

Dividends may consist of cash, shares, options or the transfer of assets or any combination thereof. ¶93. Dividends may only be declared by solvent companies and then only when such declaration does not materially prejudice the company's ability to pay its debts. ¶¶93-94.

Articles 97-100 set forth the procedures to increase or reduce share capital. A solvent company may purchase its own shares if such purchase does not affect its solvency. ¶102. Shareholder approval via a resolution passed at a general meeting is required. ¶103.

A company may not provide financial assistance for the purchase of its own shares unless it is in the business of lending money. ¶107.

Nevertheless, there are exceptions, such as where the board believes that extending such financial assistance is on reasonable grounds and is in the best interests of the company as a whole, does not affect solvency and is fair and reasonable to the company's shareholders as a whole. ¶108(1). The shareholders must agree. ¶109.

8.7 Corporate Governance

The business of the company must be managed by its board of directors. ¶132. Nevertheless, the board may delegate its powers to a committee, to a single director, to an employee or to any other person. ¶132(4).

A company must have a registered physical office where communications may be sent. It is not necessary that the company occupy the physical premises at the registered address. Incorporation services, law or accounting firms may thus provide registered offices for their corporate clients. ¶116.

Board meetings may be called by any director upon the giving of reasonable notice to other directors. Board meetings need not be conducted in person and may instead utilize any agreed upon technology. Minutes of the meeting and a record of the resolutions passed must be kept. ¶128. A quorum is composed of two directors except in those cases where a company has but a single director. ¶119.

The company's first annual general meeting must be held within eighteen months of incorporation. ¶120. The annual meeting must consider the company's annual financial report, report of directors and the auditor's report, even if such consideration is not specifically provided for. The company's auditor must attend the general meeting and field questions posed by the company's members.If the company fails to convene an annual meeting, a Myanmar court may order a meeting held. ¶120.

Provisions relating to the convening of annual meetings do not apply to "small companies"in accordance with Paragraph 120 (7). The term "small company"is defined in the law as a company having less than thirty employees and revenues under 50,000,000 kyat per annum.

Public companies and guarantee companies with a share capital must have an initial meeting no sooner than 28 days after incorporation and no later than six months after incorporation. This meeting is called a statutory meeting. Prior to the meeting, the directors shall circulate a report to the members containing that audited and certified information specified in Paragraph 121(3) of the law.

A general meeting of the company may be called for by members holding at least 10% of the voting shares. Such an extraordinary meeting will be held at the expense of the members who request it. ¶122(1)(i). Additionally, a court may order a meeting to be held on such fair and equitable terms as the court decides. Presumably this extends to the allocation of expenses for such a meeting. ¶122(1).(j)

Shareholders with at least 10% ownership or 100 individual members may request that the company's directors call a meeting. In such a circumstance, the members are not liable for the expenses of the meeting if the directors agree to call a meeting. ¶122(2). The written request for such a meeting may be presented on multiple sheets of paper. ¶122(3).

Such an extraordinary general meeting must be called within 21 days of the completed request. In case the directors fail to convene the requested meeting, the petitioners may themselves call the meeting within three months of the date of the request. ¶122(4).

Any resolution to be voted upon at the extraordinary meeting must be in writing, signed and contain a short explanatory statement. ¶122(8). This document may be provided to members in the notice of meeting as long as it is not overly long or contains defamatory matter. ¶122(9).

Meetings may be held either in person or using "any technology which is available to members."¶122(10). This is a clear statement that unless required by the company's constitution, members need not be physically present for a general or extraordinary meeting.

Paragraph 123 sets forth the time limits, notice and procedural requirements for holding a meeting. The notice must:

  (i) set out the place, date and time for the meeting;

 (ii) state the general nature of the meetings business;

(iii) set out the resolutions to be proposed at the meeting, including whether any are special resolutions or resolutions proposed by members, with any necessary explanatory material;

(iv) provide information and instructions regarding the appointment of proxies or corporate representatives, including the time by which notices of such appointments may be received and the address or number to which such notices of appointments may be sent; and

(v) include any other information required to be provided by the constitution or under this Law.

Voting may be by a show of hands, but if the chair or at least five members or 10% of the shareholders so request, a poll must be taken. ¶122(2)(d). The poll will be conducted in the manner directed by the chair or in accordance with the company's constitution.

A member may appoint a proxy to attend meetings and to exercise his rights. ¶125. A proxy must be made in accordance with the procedures specified in the law and must be received at least 48 hours in advance of any meeting. ¶125(5).

Ordinary resolutions may be passed by a simple majority; special resolutions require 75% approval. ¶126. A company with a sole director need not convene meetings and may instead pass any necessary resolutions by signing them. ¶127. Seven days after a meeting, a member may request a copy of the minutes. ¶128(7).

Directors may not vote on matters in which they have a personal interest. ¶135. If the company's constitution so permits, a director may nevertheless be present for discussions concerning such a personal interest matter even if the affected director cannot vote.

A director must disclose any personal interest. The interest of the director's family is not mentioned in the law. The phrase, "spouse, relative or associate"is used in Paragraph 157 concerning property transfers to officers. Such transfers or benefits must be approved by the members. ¶158. This phrase presumably, though not explicitly, would apply to directors as well.

Directors may not vote to exempt themselves from liability. ¶152. A company may nevertheless indemnify directors for their good faith acts. ¶153(2). A director shall not be personally liable where he has acted in good faith based on advice of counsel or expert advice. ¶163.

The board may authorize remuneration and extend loans to directors if doing so is in the best interests of the company. ¶159. Additional requirements for such benefits are set forth in the same paragraph.

A company's initial directors are those mentioned in the application for incorporation. ¶145(1). Thereafter, the directors will be appointed by an ordinary resolution at a general meeting of members. ¶145(b). Vacancies may be filled by the directors subject to approval at the next general meeting. ¶145(c). A director may be removed by an ordinary resolution passed at a member's general meeting.

The office of corporate secretary is to be filled by appointment of the board of directors. ¶151.

8.8   Jurisdiction

The Myanmar courts have jurisdiction to enter any of the following orders with respect to a company, upon the application of a member, an aggrieved individual or a person determined by the Directorate to be affected:

(a) that the company be wound up;

(b) that the company's existing constitution be modified or repealed;

(c) regulating the conduct of the companys affairs in the future;

(d) for the purchase of any shares by any member or person to whom a share in the company has been transmitted by will or by operation of law;

(e) for the purchase of shares with an appropriate reduction of the company's share capital;

(f) for the company to institute, prosecute, defend or discontinue specified proceedings;

(g) authorizing a member, or a person to whom a share in the company has been transmitted by will or by operation of law, to institute, prosecute, defend or discontinue specified proceedings in the name and on behalf of the company;

(h) appointing a receiver of any or all of the companys property;

(i) restraining a person from engaging in specified conduct or from doing a specified act;

(j) requiring a person to do a specified act; or

(k) for damages.

¶¶165,166.

General rules for such lawsuits and presumptions pertaining to them are set forth in successive paragraphs. In general the courts have plenary jurisdiction; that is, they may make any orders and give any directions considered appropriate in relation to proceedings brought or intervened in with leave, or an application for leave, including:

(a) interim orders;

(b) directions about the conduct of the proceedings, including requiring mediation;

(c) an order directing the company, or an officer of the company, to do, or not to do, any act; and

(d) an order appointing an independent person to investigate, and report to the court on:

  (i) the financial affairs of the company;

 (ii) the facts or circumstances which gave rise to the cause of action the subject of the proceedings; or

(iii) the costs incurred in the proceedings by the parties to the proceedings and the person granted leave.

¶172, ¶348.

The courts have the power to grant injunctive relief. ¶385.

8.9 Initial Public Offerings

The law contains rules concerning a company's conversion to a public company and the initial public offering. ¶¶174-190.

8.10 Marketing of Securities

The MCL also contains restrictions on the marketing of foreign securities in Myanmar. It is a little unusual to see such provisions in the MCL as normally these would be part of a country's securities laws. The restrictions do not apply to licensed securities firms in Myanmar. Companies that seek to raise funds in Myanmar without engaging a local securities firm for the purposes of marketing are thus advised to tread carefully. Road shows are prohibited by implication; door to door sales calls are specifically banned. Failure to comply may render any subscription void. See ¶191 et seq.

8.11 Accounting and Financial Records

Companies must keep books of account, financial statements and reports. ¶218. These may be kept in English. ¶219(1). Annual balance sheets must be prepared which contain a summary of the property and assets and of the capital and liabilities of the company. ¶220. If the company is a holding company, details concerning the company's subsidiaries must be included. ¶223. A copy of the company's financial statements must be forwarded to the Registrar. ¶225.

The Registrar has the authority to appoint investigators and investigate a company's records where the directors may have committed an offense or upon the petition of members owning 10% of the company's shares. ¶227 et seq.

The law contains extensive cessation of business operations provisions whether on account of insolvency, voluntary or forced liquidation. ¶245 et seq. The MCL empowers the Myanmar courts to make specific rules relating to liquidations. ¶352.

The law contains a list of penalties for violations of its provisions. It also carves out a safe harbor for directors where the director will not be liable if he shows that he:

(a) took all reasonable and proper steps to ensure that the requirements of the law were complied with;

(b) took all reasonable and proper steps to ensure that the board complied with the requirements of the law (in the case of an offense in relation to a duty imposed on the board);

(c) the director or officer (in the case of an offense in relation to a duty imposed on the director or officer) took all reasonable and proper steps to ensure that the requirements of the law were complied with; or

(d) where the director could not reasonably have been expected to take steps to ensure that either he or the board complied with the requirements of the law.

¶400

CHAPTER 9

Commencing Business

Business Structures

This chapter will be substantially affected by the imminent passage of the new Myanmar Companies Law. Parts of older legislation may apply during the transition period. Additionally, precedential guidance is useful in understanding how new structures and systems are likely to be utilized or operate.

SEVERAL LEGAL OR BUSINESS structures are available for doing business in Myanmar:

- partnerships
- limited liability companies
- branch or representative offices
- non-profit companies

The most common way of doing business in Myanmar is through a limited liability company. At the moment, the governing law for LLC's is the Companies

Act of 1914, though this will shortly change. Myanmar companies are those in which no foreigner may own a share or be a director. Otherwise, a limited liability company could be a foreign company registered in Myanmar or by means of a branch office or representative office formed outside Myanmar. Whether a company will be classified as a foreign company or not depends on the degree of foreign ownership. Rules have not yet been promulgated. The former law operated so that if a foreign partner owned at least one share, the company would be defined as a foreign company and must obtain a foreign investment license.

One of the most important points to remember is that foreigners who invest in Myanmar through nominees without obtaining a foreign investment license have no legal standing to enforce their rights. A company found to be a nominee company will be blacklisted.

Except for restricted business activities, a limited liability company may be 100% owned by foreign investors.

Partnerships formed in Myanmar under the Partnership Act of 1932 are of unlimited duration. The number of partners, however, is limited to 20. Partnerships need not be registered. Because partnerships are of unlimited duration, consent of all the partners is required to dissolve the partnership.

An undischarged bankrupt is not eligible to serve as a director of either a private or public company. Shareholders and directors need not be resident in Myanmar.

Under the new 2016 Investment Law, it is no longer necessary for all foreign companies to obtain a foreign investment license. Section 2 of the new Investment Law makes it clear that the legislation applies to all companies "incorporated in accordance with the Myanmar Companies Act or any other applicable laws, and entities incorporated in accordance with the laws of a foreign country. Foreign businesses, whether they have previously obtained a foreign investment permit or not, are subject to the Investment Law on a non-discriminatory basis. Joint ventures with the government, however, need not obtain a license. After registration, a company must obtain a Certificate of Commencement of Business in order to begin operations. Companies with state participation are subject to the Special Company Act of 1950 as well as the Companies Law. Transfer of shares of a company operating under a foreign investment license to a foreigner, foreign entity or even a Myanmar citizen must be approved by the Myanmar Investment Commission. After approval, registration of the new shareholder must be filed with the Directorate of Investment and Company Administration.

Joint ventures with Myanmar partners require the Myanmar partner to be at least a 20% partner if the business purpose is to engage in a business where foreign investment is prohibited or restricted. There are no restrictions on lending the local partner sufficient capital for the purposes of meeting the joint venture's capital requirements.

The minimum share capital required for a new domestic company formed under the Companies Law is as follows (in U.S. dollars):

Industrial, hotel and construction	150,000
Services	50,000
Travel and tourism	50,000
Bank or Insurance Rep. office	50,000

Capital requirements for foreign companies are higher:

Manufacturing	500,000
Services	300,000

The Myanmar Investment Commission can raise or lower these requirements in individual cases. However, simply because the possibility exists that the capital requirements will be lowered does not mean that the Investment Commission will do so and in some cases may require a higher capital amount.

Additionally, companies can expect to pay registration fees of roughly $2500. These amounts do not include attorneys or consultants fees for assistance with respect to formation. While these fees vary, they can commonly range from $5000 to $50,000 depending on the industry and the number of different ministerial approvals needed.

A foreign company may set up a branch under either the Companies Law or the Foreign Investment Law. If formation is sought only under the Companies Law, as would be the case where the foreign company is providing technical support to a local agent, no foreign investment license is needed. Such a branch office is not permitted to engage in trading but may provide technical assistance and marketing. Trading companies are not permitted. A foreign company will need a local agent, partner, or distributor.

Negative List

Several industries are protected and not open to foreign investment. The government may permit joint ventures either between a government owned or connected enterprise and a foreign company or a purely private domestic enterprise and a foreign company in the discretion of the Myanmar Investment Commission and the concerned ministry. The government may permit foreign companies to enter even these sectors and has done so with respect to telecom and banking. Otherwise, the following areas are restricted:

- Extraction and sale of Teak
- Cultivation and conservation of forest plantations
- Exploration, extraction and sale of hydrocarbons
- Exploration, extraction and sale of pearls, jade, gems
- Fisheries
- Postal and telecommunication sectors
- Air and railway
- Banking and insurance
- Broadcasting and television
- Exploration, extraction and export of metals
- Electricity generation, except for public-private partnerships
- Security and defense, arms

In 2016, the Myanmar Investment Commission ("MIC") published Notification 26/2016 dated 21 March 2016 ("Notification 26/2016") concerning prohibited and restricted activities for foreign investment.

While the new Notification 26/2016 is largely similar to earlier legislation, it contains important changes:

The following investments may now be 100% foreign-owned:

- Production and distribution of hybrid seeds;
- Production and propagation of high-yield seeds and local seeds;
- Manufacture of rubber and rubber products; and
- Ecotourism.

Ecotourism no longer requires the approval of the Ministry of Environmental Conservation and Forestry. Vaccine manufacture and sales may only be accomplished through a joint venture with the government.

According to the Ministerial Notification, economic activities which damage or threaten to destroy the watershed, forests, sacred religious sites, traditional ritual sites, grazing lands, plantations, farmlands, and/or water resources are prohibited.

In addition to the previous requirement that certain rail-related economic activities could only be performed through a joint venture with the Ministry of Rail Transport (which has recently been amalgamated to form the Ministry of Transport and Communication), it is now possible to engage in some of these activities through Build Operate and Transfer (BOT) projects or lease. Furthermore, the categories of rail related economic activities for which the permission of the Union Government is required have been significantly reduced, but it remains necessary to obtain the approval of the Ministry of Rail Transport (which has recently been amalgamated to form the Ministry of Transport and Communication) for all rail-related economic activities. The approval of the Ministry for Electric Power and Energy is additionally required for any generation of electric power to be used for train operations.

Permission of the Union Government is no longer required for "vehicle inspection, driving training centers, or repair and maintenance training."These activities may only be conducted through a joint venture company of which the share capital is 50% owned by Myanmar citizens.

Notification 26/2016 notes that if the MIC determines that an economic activity requires approval from another government ministry, such economic activity may not be carried out as a 100% foreign investment. This grants the MIC broad discretion to prohibit wholly foreign ownership of entities conducting economic activities which the MIC considers should require ministry approval.

Service businesses "that are not suitable as an investment"may only be conducted with the permission of the relevant ministry. While this restriction only applies to a service business that has applied for an investment permit from the MIC, as there is no guidance as to what may be considered "not suitable."This gives the MIC potentially broad discretionary powers to require service providers to seek ministry approval.

General Requirements

In order to incorporate, the company must have a registered address in Myanmar. Companies must display their name outside their registered office and the name must be contained in the corporate seal, letterhead, advertisements and any other company documentation. If the company address is changed after incorporation, notice must be given to the Directorate of Investment and Company Administration within 28 days of the change.

A general shareholder's meeting must be held annually. A new company is given a grace period of six months before holding its first general meeting; thus, a new company must hold its annual meeting within eighteen months of incorporation. Subsequent general meetings must be held during each following calendar year on an annual basis. Audited financial statements must be prepared for each annual general meeting. An annual meeting must be held within nine months of closing the annual audit.

A company must file an annual return within 21 days after the close of the annual meeting.

Extraordinary and special resolutions passed by the company must be filed with the Directorate of Investment and Company Administration within fifteen days.

Penalties have been established for noncompliance.

Applications may be rejected for minor errors. If a necessary document is on a checklist its absence will not be overlooked. While the ministries make a good faith effort to comply with the time limits contained in the legislation, the foreign investor cannot always rely on ministry compliance. Usually the application proceedings are a process of give and take with the various ministries having jurisdiction. For this reason, it is impossible to say with any certainty how quickly the process can be completed. An investor should expect the entire process to take from two months to over a year.

Procedural Requirements

There are many steps to complete before a new company can be successfully formed in Myanmar. Some of the steps appear simple but are actually somewhat involved. Obtaining a Certificate of Commencement of Business sounds simple enough, but to obtain one you have to first obtain a foreign investment license as well as register the company under the Companies Act. Thus, often a single step includes many intermediate steps.

Previously, in all cases it was necessary to submit a proposal to the Myanmar Investment Commission. ("MIC") While formally a proposal is no longer required in all cases, preparing a proposal is a good idea in case the Commission decides to require one. The Commission has fifteen days to decide whether or not to accept the filing of the proposal and then 90 days to determine whether or not the application will be accepted. The Commission may accept the proposal as filed or modify it. If a proposal addresses a subject matter within the jurisdiction of another Myanmar government ministry, that ministry must give its approval as well. The Commission will consult with the relevant region or state government as well as the Ministry of Forestry and Environmental Conservation to obtain their recommendations concerning the environmental and social impact of the proposal. The local governments and the environmental ministry have seven days to respond to this consultation request. Other ministries whose input is needed are similarly granted a seven-day period from their request of the relevant consultation. As in most other countries, these time limits are often aspirational.

Evaluation of License Application

An application for a foreign investment license is evaluated taking into account the following factors:

(a) whether the proposal is compatible with the policies adopted by the Foreign Investment Law;

(b) assessment of financial trustworthiness based on the following information;

    (i) bank statements;

    (ii) latest audit report;

    (iii) company business development report;

(c) Economic justification based on the following:

    (i) estimated annual net profit;

    (ii) estimated annual income and foreign currency expenditure;

    (iii) investment recoupment period;

    (iv) potential jobs created;

(v) enhancement of GDP;

(vi) local and export market assessment;

(vii) local consumption;

(d) technical assessment of industrial technology;

(e) environmental assessment by the Department of Environmental Conservation;

(f) potential public and private sector social impact;

(g) compliance with existing law.

If a license is granted, the foreign investor then must form an entity to conduct business within the terms of the foreign investment license. If the Commission approves the investment, the next step is to submit the required documentation for corporate formation at the Directorate of Investment and Company Administration. The Directorate may issue a temporary registration until the formalities are completed in order to speed the formation process. However, this temporary registration may not be used to commence business activities. If the investment license contemplates any construction, the project must be completed within the timeframe set forth in the license. There are provisions for extensions, but an extension may not exceed 50% of the original time estimated for project completion except in case of *force majeure*. If construction is not promptly commenced or completed, the license may be withdrawn.

The licensee must file quarterly reports with the Commission.

Contents of Business Proposal

A business proposal must contain the following:

(a) name of the investor or promoter, citizenship, address, business location, corporate certificate of good standing, location of head office of effective management, location of incorporated business organization, type of business;

(b) facts contained in clause (a) include persons participating in the joint venture if the investment is formed as joint venture;

(c) documents related to clause (a) or (b);

(d) business and financial records of the investor, promoter or joint venture partner;

(e) facts related to manufacturing or service business;

(f) duration of investment and construction period;

(g) proposed location of the new business in the Union;

(h) technical know-how to be used;

(i) type and volume of energy consumption;

(j) quantity and value of required main machinery, equipment, raw materials and similar materials to be used in business during the construction period;

(k) required area and type of land;

(I) annual profit/loss projections;

(m) annual required foreign currency requirements and estimated foreign currency income;

(n) estimated annual local and export sales;

(o) economic justification;

(p) environmental protection measures;

(q) type of investment in the Union;

(r) if formation of a partnership is contemplated, the draft contract, share ratio and amount of the shares to be contributed by the partners, ratio for allocation of profit and duties and responsibilities of the partners;

(s) if formation of a limited liability company is desired, the draft contract, shareholders agreement and articles of association, authorized capital of the company, type of shares, amount of capital to be contributed by the shareholders;

(t) name, citizenship, address and designation of the directors for the investment organization;

(u) total paid up capital, ratio of local to foreign capital contribution and total foreign capital invested;

(v) an undertaking to comply with the terms of the license;

(w) the draft land lease agreement should accompany the business plan.

(x) social and environmental impact study.

(y) for natural resource based business, evidence of submission and approval by the concerned Union ministry.

If a foreign investment license is granted, the next step is to register the new company.

Documents Required

The required documents to register a company are the following:

1. Form A of the Myanmar Companies Regulation 1957;
2. Memorandum and Articles of Association (Copy);
3. Duly completed questionnaire form;
4. Intended activities to be performed;
5. Estimated expenditures to be incurred in Myanmar for the first year's operations;
6. Financial stability of the company/individual;
7. Board of Directors resolution, if the subscriber is a company;
8. A copy of the Permit and the Decision of the MIC for manufacturing, hotel and construction businesses;
9. Statement concerning whether a shareholder or director is a shareholder or director at another company;
10. Undertaking not to engage in trading;
11. Identification documents for each shareholder and director.

In the case of a foreign branch/representative office, the following shall be furnished in addition to the above-mentioned documents:

(1) Instead of the company's Memorandum and Articles of Association, a copy of the corporate parent's

Memorandum and Articles of Association or other instruments constituting or defining the constitution of the company, duly notarized and consularized by the Myanmar Embassy concerned in the country where the company is incorporated;

(2) The Annual Report for the last two fiscal (or) in the case of the corporate parent, the balance sheet and profit and loss accounts for the last two fiscal years, duly notarized and consularized by the Myanmar Embassy concerned in the country of incorporation;

(3) Where the original memorandum and Articles of Association and other relevant documents are not in the English language, authentication of the translation into English.

The application for Registration is to be accompanied by the following documents:

(1) Two sets containing copies of the memorandum and Articles of Association duly stamped and printed both in Burmese and English;

(2) Certificate of Good Standing;

(3) Certification of copies of the documents;

(4) Declaration concerning the location of registered office;

(5) Translation certificate issued by a qualified translator;

(6) List of directors;

(7) List of person(s) authorized to accept service of process and notices in Myanmar on behalf of the company (i.e. for a branch office of a foreign company);

(8) A copy of Permit & Decision of the Myanmar Investment Commission for the Manufacturing, Hotel & Construction businesses;

(9) A copy of the identification documents for each shareholder and director;

(10) An undertaking not to engage in trading.

For a public company, the following additional documents shall be submitted before commencing business:

(1) List of directors;

(2) Director's undertaking to acquire qualification shares.

CHAPTER 10

Taxation

THE KINGS OF BURMA IMPOSED a tax called the *ngay-daw*, or "royal silver" as their principal source of revenue. It was a house tax, similar to a property tax. The next tax imposed was a tax on production. An acre was assumed to produce a certain number of crops and a portion of these was destined for the public treasury. When Burma came under British control, the British introduced a ten percent duty on imports.

Amendments to Myanmar's tax regime have been long-awaited. On March 24, 2014, the Union Government enacted two new tax laws with immediate effect. These are the *Law Amending the Income Tax Law*, Pyihtaungsu Hluttaw Law No. 15/2014 and the *Law Amending the Commercial Tax Law*, Pyihtaungsu Hluttaw Law No. 16/2014. On March 28, 2014 a third tax law, the *Tax of the Union Law*, Pyihtaungsu Hluttaw Law No. 20/2014, was enacted as well. These are supplemented by notifications from the Internal Revenue Department. The new laws clarify exemptions and tax rates charged as well as specifying tax recordkeeping and administrative requirements. Under the Foreign Investment Law, tax benefits granted to existing companies will continue only for those companies actively engaged in the export trade. This does not, however, eliminate tax advantages granted by other laws.

Tax rates can change annually in Myanmar. The Union Tax Law 2015, Pyidaungsu Hluttaw Law No. 17, 2 April 2015, modified tax rates for the 2015 and following fiscal years. A company's tax year is its financial year, normally from April 1 to March 31. Tax returns should be filed within three months of the close of the fiscal year. Advance tax payments must be made in monthly or quarterly installments based on a calculation of estimated tax owed. Employees covered by tax withholding need not file a return.

Capital gains tax must be paid within one month of the sale of the asset.

An employer must also file a declaration of salaries paid to the authorities within three months of the close of the tax year. Employers with five or more employees must provide benefits under the Social Security Law of 1954.

When a company goes out of business it must file its final return within one month of ceasing operations.

The tax statute of limitations is three years. This prescriptive period does not apply in cases of fraud. In those cases, a company's returns can be re-assessed. Failure to file timely returns or cooperate with the Myanmar tax authorities constitutes fraud under the law. Given this broad definition, the statute of limitations is hardly a safe harbor. Problems could arise where the authorities decide to audit past years' returns, even if these are outside the prescriptive period. In cases of fraud, the additional tax owed must be paid along with a 50% penalty.

Income not Subject to Taxation

The *Law Amending the Income Tax Law* specifies that certain types of income are not subject to income taxation. These are:

1. Income received by any religious or charitable organization and used exclusively for matters of religion or charity;

2. Income received by a local authority;

3. Proceeds of the commutation of a pension, condolence payments [which otherwise would have to be] categorized as "salary";

4. Compensation obtained for death or injury;

5. Insurance proceeds;

6. Income of a casual, nonrecurring nature with the following exceptions:

    (i) capital gains;

    (ii) income from an enterprise;

7. Share of the aftertax profit of an association.

Tax exemptions granted in the Foreign Investment Law are confirmed.

The payor of monies subject to tax is required to withhold estimated tax due and forward it to the Ministry of Finance. Failure to withhold taxes due is subject to fines and penalties. If there is a failure to file a return the Ministry may nonetheless assess income tax. The Revenue Office of the Ministry of Finance is vested with the same enforcement powers as a civil court.

Commercial Tax Law

The second of these revenue laws is the *Law Amending the Commercial Tax Law*. The *Commercial Tax Law* in Myanmar is a revenue-raising measure similar, but not identical, to the well-known value-added tax (VAT). Unlike VAT, it applies only to those transactions specified in the law, though on a wide range of goods and services. Commercial tax is charged at the rate of 5% on general trading and the domestic sale of imported goods. ¶11(d).

The tax is imposed on anyone engaged in manufacturing, distribution, importation of goods, trading or the provision of services. The tax is to be paid by the manufacturer, importer, trader or service provider. ¶5. In order to leave Myanmar, a person must obtain a tax clearance from the Ministry of Finance. It is not clear how this provision will be applied in practice, though it is common in many countries.

Commercial Tax Rates

The third and perhaps most important law, the *Tax of the Union Law*, sets forth the tax rates for the major taxes imposed in the Union. The Commercial Tax rates are as follows

General goods	5%
Cigarettes	120%
Other tobacco	60%
Alcohol	60%
Wine	50%
Teak, hardwood logs	25%
Jade and gemstones(uncut)	15%
Jewelry	5%
Vehicles with +1800cc motor	25%
Gasoline, diesel, avgas	10%
Natural gas	8%

The Commercial Tax charged on the import of the above goods must not be set off from the commercial tax charged on the proceeds of their sale. Likewise, the commercial tax charged when purchasing these goods must not be set off from the commercial tax charged on the proceeds of the resale of these goods. ¶11(e).

Services Tax

There is a 5% tax on services. The following activities are exempt:

a. Real estate brokerage

b. Car parks brokerage

c. Life insurances

d. Microfinance

e. Health care except body fitness

f. Education

g. Transportation of goods

h. Employment agencies

i. Banking

j. Customs clearance

k. Party Rentals

l. Contract manufacturing

m. Funeral-related

n. Container Transport

o. Child care

p. Traditional Massage, or massage by a blind person

q. Moving service

r. Service for which a road toll is charged

s. Veterinary

t. Public sanitation

u. Air transport

v. Cultural

w. Public transportation (bus, railway, and ferry)

The provision of information technology and management consultancy services are no longer exempt from this tax. ¶11(f). The services tax from non-exempt activities is 5%.

The sale of developed real estate, i.e, structures, is subject to a 5% tax. ¶11(g).

With respect to the sale of goods, provision of services or trading, commercial tax is not assessed unless the company has sales in excess of Ks. 20,000,000 annually. Previously the exemption threshold was Ks. 15,000,000 per annum. ¶12.

Taxes are assessed and payable in national currency.

Commercial Tax on Exports

Commercial tax on exports is at the following rates:

General	0%
Crude oil	5%
Natural gas	8%
Teak, hardwood logs	50%
Jade and gemstones (uncut)	15%
Jewelry	5%
Electrical Power	5%

Note that the rate on jade and jewelry has almost been halved and the general tax on exports has dropped from 5% to zero.

Avjet fuel is subject to a commercial tax of 5%.

No commercial tax may be charged on the following:

(1) Paddy, rice, split, soft-/rough bran, paddy husk

(2) Wheat grain and flour

(3) Maize and other cereals

(4) Pulses, whether milled or split and powdered

(5) Groundnuts

(6) Sesame

(7) Mustard, sunflower, tamarind and cotton seeds

(8) Oil Palm

(9) Cotton (various types)

(10) Jute and other fibers

(11) Garlic, onions

(12) Potatoes

(13) Cassava plant or powder

(14) Spices, Prepared spices

(15) Fresh fruits

(16) Vegetables

(17) Sugarcane, sugar

(18) Mulberry leaves

(19) Medicinal plants or herbs

(20) Thatch, reeds and misc. agricultural products

(21) Firewood, bamboo

(22) Live animals, fish and prawns

(23) Silk cocoons

(24) Cane, finished or unfinished

(25) Honey and bee wax

(26) Lac

(27) Residue of groundnuts, sesame, cottonseeds, rice, bran

(28) Soap stocks, soap powder

(29) Bleaching substances (of oil residue)

(30) Coir yarn, coconut shell charcoal

(31) Tea leaves, pickled or dried

(32) Stamps, including revenue stamps

(33) Sealing wax and sticks

(34) Slate, slate pencils, chalk

(35) Fish sauces

(36) Groundnut, sesame, sunflower oil, rice bran edible oil soybean oil, oil cakes

(37) Fresh frish, prawns, meat

(38) Milk

(39) Chili, chili powder

(40) Saffron, saffron powder

(41) Ginger

(42) Fish paste

(43) Ripe tamarind

(44) National flag

(45) Beads

(46) Rulers, erasers sharpeners

(47) Firewood alternatives

(48) Coconut oil (not palm oil)

(49) Poultry eggs

(50) Pumpkin and watermelon seeds, cashew nuts

(51) Religious clothes

(52) Oil dregs

(53) Salt

(54) Rubber paste

(55) Betel nuts

(56) Fertilizer

(57) Insecticides and fungicides

(58) Farm equipment and parts

(59) Animal feed

(60) Animal medicines

(61) Animal breed

(62) Solar panels and accessories

(63) X-ray film and equipment

(64) Bandages and surgical supplies

(65) Medicines (except those prohibited/restricted)

(66) Drugs

(67) Textbooks and School Supplies

(68) Graphite for pencils

(69) Condoms

(70) State defense and military equipment

(71) Gun powder and dynamite for civil use

(72) Crops, seeds, nursery plants

(73) Printing fees from Ministry of Defense security printing, military weapons, spare parts, vehicles

(74) Firetrucks, hearses

(75) Duty free material to be sold to overseas passengers

(76) Goods used by diplomats and embassy staff

(77) Goods purchased for consumption by armed forces

(78) Raw material or parts of goods provided by non-resident supplier for use on a CMP basis and goods for wrapping the finished product

(79) Fuel sold to foreign embassies and organizations by the Ministry of Energy

Imports Exempt from Commercial Tax

Commercial tax is not levied on the following imported goods:

(a) Fertilizers

(b) Insecticides, pesticides, fungicides, etc.

(c) Farm equipment, farm machines and machine parts

(d) Fish feed, shrimp feed (raw material, finished goods)

(e) Animal feed (raw material, finished goods)

(f) Animal medicines

(g) Breeding livestock

(h) Solar panels, solar charge controllers and solar inverters

(i) X-ray films and plates and other X-ray, surgical, medicinal or pharmaceutical apparatus and equipment

(j) Bandages, gauze, other surgical dressing material, hospital and surgical outfit and sundries

(k) Pharmaceuticals and other medicines (except medicine restricted by rules and regulations)

(l) Drugs

(m) Textbooks, exercise and drawing books of various kinds and papers for the production of such books and all sorts of pencils

(n) Graphite for the production of pencils

(o) Condoms

(p) Defense and military equipment

(q) Civilian use munitions and demolition equipment

(r) Crop seeds, nursery plants

Income Tax Rates

Personal

Income tax rates remain the same and have been established as follows (in kyat):

1-2 million	0%
2-5 million	5%
5-10 million	10%
10-20 million	15%
20-30 million	20%
Over 30 million	25%

Net rental income is charged separately at the rate of 10%. ¶20.

The basic deduction for a married parent is Ks. 1 million; Ks. 1 million for a spouse and Ks. 500,00 for a child. The family deduction is thus Ks. 2.5 million for a family with one child.

A foreigner who works part of the year in Myanmar but who resides abroad is taxed at the rate of 3.5%. If the Myanmar-source income is paid in a currency other than kyat the tax must be paid in the currency in which the income was earned.

Overseas Burmese citizens pay at a rate of 10% after application of the standard deduction, which is 20% of income but may not exceed 10 million Ks. for a single tax year. There is an additional spousal deduction of 500,000 Ks. and a 300,000 Ks. deduction for each child.

The law creates new tax rates for income which has escaped assessment. The rates start at 3% for amounts less than Ks.100,000,000 with a ceiling of 30% in the highest bracket. ¶24.

Corporate

Companies formed under Myanmar law are taxed at a rate of 25%. New businesses may be eligible for a tax holiday if their income does not exceed 10 million Ks. for three years in a row. The previous threshold was half that amount.

Capital Gains

There is a 10% capital gains tax except with respect to capital gains earned in the oil and gas sector. These are taxed at substantially higher and regressive rates (in billions of kyat):

0-100	40%
100-150	45%
150 and above	50%

The rates here remain unchanged.

Capital gains of less than 10,000,000 Ks. in a single year are exempt from tax. This is double the previous amount. Funds paid as a reward for reporting certain types of crime are exempt from tax as are international awards, such as the Nobel Prize. State lottery winnings are also exempt.

10.0.1   Other Taxes

Customs duties are not a recent phenomena. Even before the British took control, all vessels arriving in Burma had to make a declaration of their cargo. Any merchandise not included in the declaration was considered contraband and seized. A levy of 12.5% was levied on the declared goods. Ten percent was destined for the emperor and 2.5% to be shared by the lesser nobility.

Customs duties today are imposed in accordance with the Customs Tariff of Myanmar Law (2012). Today the rates are variable. Customs exemptions may be granted for materials and machinery imported in order to expand a business. There is similarly an exemption from tax on goods produced for export.

There are no controlled foreign company rules or transfer pricing regulations. Royalties, management fees and interest charges paid to affiliates are deductible as long as they are consistent with the size of the business. There is no group taxation. There are no thin capitalization rules. There is no specific debt to equity ratio safe harbor, though one may be introduced in the future.

Stamp duty is imposed on real estate transfers and other transactions such as share transfers, bonds, and in inheritance matters. If the particular transaction is denominated in dollars, the rate is 1%. There is an excise tax on alcohol.

Myanmar has tax treaties with Bangladesh, India,

Indonesia, Laos, Malaysia, Singapore, Korea, Thailand, the United Kingdom and Viet Nam.

Tax Collection by Ministries

There is more than one tax collector in Myanmar. Eleven separate ministries are responsible for the collection of different types of taxes assessed on individuals and business. These are as follows:

1. Ministry of Home Affairs: Property tax
2. Ministry of Agriculture and Irrigation: Water tax
3. Ministry of Home Affairs: Embankment tax
4. Ministry of Environmental Conservation and Forestry: Tax on extraction of forest materials
5. Ministry of Home Affairs: Tax on extraction of minerals
6. Ministry of Livestock & Fisheries and Rural Development: Natural pond and lake tax
7. Ministry of Environmental Conservation and Forestry: Rubber paste tax
8. Ministry of Energy: Production of oil and natural gas tax
9. Ministry of Mining: Mineral tax and gemstone tax
10. Ministry of Communications, Information and Technology: Tax on telecommunications Services
11. Ministry of Electrical Power: Electricity tax

CHAPTER 11

Banking and Insurance

HISTORICALLY, THE BURMESE DID NOT USE coins or paper money. In the 16th century the King of Burma made an unsuccessful effort to establish a currency. For commercial transactions, gold and silver bullion were preferred. Scales were a necessary feature of shops. Lead often was mixed with silver and was considered an inferior precious metal, as was tin. In this environment swindlers prospered; at least one was executed after a failed effort to steal the King's gold. The imposition of British law brought with it the application of the Statute of 5 Henry IV, which made it a felony to "multiply gold or silver, or to use the art of multiplication."

It was once said that "Burmese have no bankers". Banking has historically been seen as somewhat suspicious and bankers did not hold high social standing. For religious reasons, hoarding was considered improper conduct. In the absence of any kind of banking tradition, Indian moneylenders and other informal networks quickly filled the commercial field. The people dealt in cash and saw no reason to have a bank account. The result is that for years the country has had a cash economy. Deposits are low and the number of borrowers per capita is amongst the lowest in the world.

Given this historical foundation, it is no surprise that constructing a modern banking system has been difficult. In 1963 the banks were nationalized. For almost fifty years Myanmar has been outside world banking.

The Burmese government has initiated banking and economic reforms. In October 2011, 11 private banks were allowed to trade foreign currency. On April 2, 2012, Burma's multiple exchange rates were abolished and the Central Bank of Myanmar established a managed float of the Burmese kyat. The bank is the sole authority to issue Myanmar's currency and this authority, at least in theory, is to be exercised autonomously without government pressure.

The Foreign Exchange Management Law 2012 removed exchange restrictions. The result was an increase in the use of the kyat for everyday transactions and the practical elimination of a currency black market. The Central Bank of Myanmar Law was signed on July 21, 2013 to create an independent Central Bank and to remove the institution administratively from the Ministry of Finance and Revenue. The new law gives the Central Bank authority to set monetary policy. The new law is also designed to shore-up and modernize the banking system so as to bring stability and with it, access to badly needed foreign capital.

The Central Bank was tasked with regulating the banking sector, the country's capital markets and the management of foreign currency reserves. The Central Bank can print money and so fund any budget deficit. In the past this led to a great disparity between the official and black market exchange rates for the kyat. These differences have largely been eliminated along with the restrictions previously in place that made it difficult for Myanmar's citizens to obtain foreign currency. Inflation currently is at 4.7%. Whether this increases or decreases depends not only on the conservatism of the central bankers, but also on the countrys economic success.

The Government's Banking Sector Development Strategy was introduced in 2012 and proposed the following reforms:

- Domestic private banks may conclude joint ventures with foreign banks
- Foreign banks permitted to establish 100% local subsidiaries
- Foreign banks allowed to open branch offices

Normally, loans made by Myanmar banks are for short periods. U Win Shein, the Union's previous Minister of Finance says that "Myanmars banks are not yet fully matured in asset and liability management and liquidity forecasting."[1] Under these conditions, long-term financing is a risk.

Currently there are twenty-eight licensed local banks. Four are state-owned:

- Myanmar Economic Bank
- Myanmar Agricultural and Development Bank
- Myanmar Investment and Commercial Ban
- Myanmar Foreign Trade Bank

The licensed private banks are:

- Myanmar Citizens Bank
- First Private Bank
- Yadanabon Bank
- Myawaddy Bank
- Yangon City Bank
- Yoma Bank
- Myanmar Oriental Bank
- Asia-Yangon Bank
- Tun Foundation
- Kanbawza Bank
- Myanma Industrial Development Bank
- Global Treasure Bank
- Sibin Tharyar Yay Bank
- Innwa Bank
- Co-Operative Bank
- Asia Green Devel-

---

[1]Quoted in *The Report: Myanmar 2014*, Oxford Business Group

- opment Bank
- Ayeyarwaddy Bank
- United Amara Bank
- Myanma Apex Bank
- Nay Pyi Taw Development Bank
- Myanmar Micro Finance Bank
- Construction and Housing Development Bank
- Small & Medium Industrial Development Bank
- Rural Development Bank

Among the banks that have opened representative offices in Myanmar are the following[2] :

- United Overseas Bank
- Overseas Chinese Banking Corporation
- Malayan Banking Berhad (Maybank)
- Bangkok Bank Public Company
- National Bank Ltd.
- Brunei Investment Bank
- First Overseas Bank
- First Commercial Bank (Singapore)
- CIMB Bank Berhad
- Sumitomo Mitsui Banking Corp.
- DBS Bank
- Tokyo-Mitsubishi Bank UFJ
- Vietnam Investment and Development Bank

---

[2]As of July, 2014, the number of banks with representative offices has increased to forty-two.

- AB Bank
- Industrial and Commercial Bank of China
- Mizuho Corporate Bank
- Siam Commercial Bank
- Woori Bank
- HSBC

Seven banks had been on the U.S. government SDN (specially-designated nationals) list, effectively prevents U.S. nationals and U.S. businesses from dealing with them. With the removal of U.S. sanctions, this is no longer the case.

In October, 2014, the Central Bank announced that nine foreign lenders would be awarded licenses:

- Australia & New Zealand Banking Group (Australia)
- Bank of Tokyo (Japan)
- Sumitomo Mitsui Banking Corp. (Japan)
- Mizuho Bank Ltd. (Japan)
- Bangkok Bank (Thailand)
- Industrial & Commercial Bank of China (China)
- Malayan Banking Bhd. (Malaysia)
- United Overseas Bank (Singapore)
- Overseas-Chinese Banking Corp. (Singapore)

In March, 2016, four new foreign banks were added to the list:

- Bank for Investment and Development of Vietnam
- State Bank of India
- Sun Commercial Bank (Taiwan)
- Shinhan Bank (South Korea)

The Microfinance Law authorized small lending operations and there are now more than 150 microfinance organizations.

Previously, tourists and other visitors were forced to purchase Foreign Exchange Certificates in order to legally obtain local currency. This requirement has been abolished and now most banks conduct currency exchange operations. Under the Foreign Exchange Management Law, all foreign exchange transactions go through authorized banks. Exchange rates are now commonly quoted for the Euro, and U.S. and Singapore dollars. Foreign companies licensed under the Foreign Investment Law may open local bank accounts.

Starting in 2015, the Central Bank of Myanmar discouraged the use of foreign currency as a medium of exchange in Myanmar. The issuance of two supervisory letters, Letter 904/2015 dated 28 May 2015 and Letter No. FE-10/365 restricts the acceptance of foreign currency for everyday transactions.

International ATM's began arriving in the country in early 2012. MasterCard and Visa began providing services to local banks. China Unionpay was connected to the network the same year. These are important developments since previously tourists had to carry cash.

Insurance

Prior to nationalization in 1963, there were seventy independent insurance companies operating in Myanmar. After a sixty-year absence, twelve foreign insurance companies representative offices were licensed in 2013. State-owned Myanmar Insurance and twelve other private insurers have as of yet no foreign competition. Government-operated Myanmar Insurance continues to be the most significant insurer in Myanmar. Unlike the banking sector, where local banks had no access to foreign capital and foreign lenders could not extend joint credit facilities to local borrowers, Myanmar insurers have always re-insured internationally. The target date for foreign insurers to begin writing local policies is 2015. Insurance in Myanmar is not as popular as in other countries. There are some unusual local insurance products on offer, such as snakebite insurance.

The explosive growth of the country's economy has created capacity and staffing issues for Myanmar Insurance.

CHAPTER 12

Employment Law

SEVERAL NEW LABOR LAWS have been passed in Myanmar. The 2008 Constitution obligated the Union to "enact necessary laws to protect the rights of workers."The Union did so with a new employment law that took effect on December 1, 2013. The terms "employer"and "employee"are defined expansively. Two laws were added in 2014, the Law Amending the Settlement of Labour Disputes Law 2014 and the Law Amending the Leave and Holidays Act (2014). Older laws addressing labor matters include the *Workmen's Compensation Act* (1923) (on the job injuries); *Shops and Establishments Act of 1951* (which established working hours), the *Leave and Holiday Act of 1952*, which provided a regime for earned leave, the *Factories Act* (1951), the *Social Security Act of 1954*, the *Employment and Training Act* (1950); the *Labor Organization Law* (2012), and the *Labour Dispute Settlement Law* (2012). New laws often do not specifically repeal older legislation which remains in force. Ministerial Notifications are issued from time to time to address lacunae or ambiguities in the law.

The Foreign Investment Law has its own guidelines with respect to employment by a foreign enterprise. The 2016 Investment Law grants investors the right to employ foreign nationals and eliminates the restrictions on the number of foreign employees employed.

The Myanmar Labor, Employment and Social Security Ministry has drafted a model employment contract for use in the country.

For businesses with more than fifteen employees, the minimum wage has been established at the rate of 450 kiyat per hour or 3600 kiyat for eight hour's wages in accordance with Notification No. 2/2015 issued by the National Minimum Wage Committee. Employers must also pay into a fund established by the Social Security Law on behalf of employees.

There are a few constitutional provisions as well. Equal pay for equal work is mandated by the constitution. However, the requirement that similarly qualified foreign and Myanmar employees must be paid the same salary has been eliminated by the 2016 Investment Law. Though only applying to government employees, there can be no discrimination on the basis of race, birth, religion or sex, but it is permitted to appoint men "to positions that are suitable for men only."A private employer would be wise to heed these restrictions. The Union is obligated to take action to reduce unemployment, but what these actions might be is not spelled out.

The law contemplates cooperation amongst the employer, employee and Labor Ministry for the purposes of identifying employment opportunities and training employees. Employers should report job vacancies to the Ministry.

Labor Contract

A written labor contract should be entered into by and between the parties within 30 days. The labor agreement should address, at a minimum, twenty-one separate categories.

These are:

1. The type of employment;
2. The probation period;
3. Wage, salary;
4. Location of the employment;
5. The term of the agreement;
6. Working hours;
7. Days off, holidays and leave;
8. Overtime;
9. Meal arrangement during the work hour;
10. Accommodation;
11. Medical treatment;
12. Transportation to and from the worksite;
13. Local rules to be followed by the employees;
14. If the employee is sent to attend the training, the limited time agreed by the employee to continue to work after

attending the train-
ing;

15. Resignation from or
termination of ser-
vice;

16. Expiration of the
agreement;

17. Obligations as stip-
ulated in the agree-
ment;

18. The cancellation of
employment agree-
ment by mutual
agreement;

19. Other matters;

20. Reference to legal
regulations which
may amend or sup-
plement the agree-
ment;

21. Miscellaneous.

Labor contracts that were entered into prior to 2013 are grandfathered. Training of employees is an important aspect of the new law and employers must im-
plement training programs in line with policies to be implemented by the Ministry of Labor. A fund will also by established by the Ministry for promoting employee training. Employer contributions to this fund will be made at a rate of .005% of payroll. Employment agencies must be licensed. A person who provides false work credentials is guilty of a criminal offense.

An employer who does not comply with the terms of a signed employment contract is guilty of a misde-
meanor. In some countries, the failure of domestic or foreign companies to pay salaries has become a perva-
sive problem and many governments seem incapable of solving the problem. The Union Government has taken an innovative approach that, at the very least, will get

the employer's attention. It should be noted that there is a reciprocal obligation imposed on the employee to comply with the terms of a signed labor agreement as well.

Recruiting foreign employees requires compliance with other laws.

Foreign unskilled workers cannot be employed by the foreign enterprise. Foreign skilled workers can be employed but the number of Myanmar workers should increase so that at least 25% of the workforce consists of Myanmar employees within two years after business commencement. This rate should increase so that by the fourth year 50% of the workforce consists of Myanmar nationals and 75% by the sixth year. The Ministry may change these percentages or extend the time for compliance when required.

There is no restriction on the number of expatriate employees, but approvals must be obtained for all. Because a foreign investor may form a company without a permit from the Myanmar Investment Commission, it follows that the situation of foreign directors of such companies has been regularized. Previously, foreigners could not be directors of companies formed without a foreign investment license under the Myanmar Companies Law.

For any position, preference is to be given to Myanmar nationals. Requests for appointment of technicians and experts can be made to the Myanmar Investment Commission. The first step in hiring foreign experts or technicians is making an application to the MIC advising the number needed. Then, after the permit is granted, applications must be made to the Directorate of Labour under the Ministry of Labour, Employment and Social Security, and for visas to the Immigration and National Registration Department under the Ministry of Immigration and Population. At the same time, provisions must be made to ensure that Myanmar national employees are properly trained so that they are eligible for advancement.

Any business with more than 30 workers must form a Worker's Coordinating Committee with two members elected by the workers and two nominated by the employer. The Coordinating Committee shall negotiate the conditions of employment and address issues relating to occupational safety, health and productivity. The Committee consists of four members. Two are chosen by the employees and two by the employer. Workplace disputes in the first instance should be resolved by the Coordinating Committee.

Grievances shall be settled by the employer within five days. At the end of the period, if a dispute cannot be resolved through direct negotiations with the affected grievant or through the Workplace Coordinating Committee, the dispute shall be forwarded to the Dispute Settlement Arbitration Body and Arbitration Council in the relevant region or state. The Council should render its decision within seven days. If the decision is unfavorable, except for essential services, the employees may strike.

Workers may not be obligated to work more than 44 hours per week and no more that eight hours per day. Any work over these hours must be paid at double rates for overtime. Office workers may work a maximum of 48 hours per week and no more than 8 hours per day.

Employees who have finished their labor contracts are entitled to an end of service benefit or severance pay. The amount of the severance is based on seniority. An employee who works less than three months is entitled to one month's wage as severance. Two months are paid when the employee completes a year or a portion of the year greater than three months. An employee with up to three years' tenure is entitled to three months salary and an employee with more than three years' tenure is entitled to five months' salary.

The Foreign Investment Law also imposes the requirement of ocmpensation for job-related injuries. Companies undergoing financial difficulties must nevertheless pay workers during any period of business cessation and a company desiring to go out of business altogether must first pay employees under the 2016 Investment Law.

Chapter 16 of the Special Economic Zones law deals with labor matters but it does not appear that there are any special exemptions granted under the law. In fact the law references the applicability of Union labor laws currently in force.

Labor Organizations

The *Labour Organization Law of 2011* (The Pyi-daungsu Hluttaw Law No. 7 / 2011) recognizes an employee's right to join a labor organization. A labor organization can be established at a workplace if thirty employees agree. Workers who are employed by employers with less than thirty employees may join with other established labor organizations. Labor organizations have separate juristic personality and may sue and be sued in their own name. Labor organizations may affiliate with each other and with international labor organizations as well. Labor organizations may represent employees in the case of labor grievances and an employee may not be terminated based on his exercise of the right to join a labor organization. Labor organizations may engage in collective bargaining. The law contemplates that a labor organization may call a strike or carry out other collective activities.

Employees at public utilities may not strike without protecting the right of the public to basic services. These fundamental services include water, electricity, fire protection, health and telecommunications. The law also recognizes that a non-essential service may become essential due to the length of a strike or a lockout.

Strikes are illegal unless the procedures set forth in the law are followed. Strikes must be approved at the national level by the labor federation. A sympathy strike, that is, a strike for political or other purposes that is not over wages or other conditions of employment is illegal. Labor organizations may not go on strike while labor arbitration is pending.

The labor organization may collect and deposit dues from employees. The dues may not exceed 2% of salary. Joining a labor organization is not mandatory. The employer must recognize a labor organization formed in accordance with the law. An employee who is active in labor matters at a workplace should not spend more than two days per month on labor matters unless the employer has otherwise agreed. These two days will count as if the employee had performed his other, non-labor related work duties. The Trade Unions Act of 1926 was specifically repealed.

CHAPTER 13

Mining

MYANMAR IS HOME TO VAST AND untouched reserves of minerals and metals, such as gold, tungsten and copper. It is also known for its reserves of precious stones and lithium. One of the world's rarest gems, painite, is found only in Myanmar.

It has been long recognized that the country has significant reserves of gems and hydrocarbons. Profitable gold sands were found near Rangoon and this led to the growth of the city. The existence of gold sands implied the existence of gold veins in the mountains up-country. Silver is mined in the north near the Chinese province of Yunnan. Even during the British colonial period, Chinese laborers worked the silver mines. Burmese pagodas are gilt with gold, so gold had to be mined for their construction and maintenance.

The mine operators did not always know what they had:

"Near these mines, crystals of different colours are found, with which the Chinese

151

> make little idols and other toys. There is
> one species of a green colour, thought to
> be the emerald."[1]

The American president, Herbert Hoover, made a fortune in zinc mining in Burma before the First World War.

Since under the 2008 Constitution, the state is the ultimate owner or all natural resources, the Union government has an obligation to enact laws to supervise their extraction and use. That, and because mining has historically been one of the country's greatest sources of wealth, has led to a significant amount of bureaucracy and red tape. Foreign firms are welcome to participate in exploration and extraction. But companies must pay royalties, land rent, corporate tax, value added tax, as well as sign a production-sharing contract. Many companies say the fees are too high.

Myanmar has also been criticized for letting activity in the mining sector despoil the land. For this reason, Myanmar wants to join the Extractive Industries Transparency Initiative. The Union's efforts in this area are well advanced.

According to Harvard University, the amount of jade and some other minerals available have been understated by billions of dollars in calculating GDP and in the reporting of exports. A ton of jade costs less

---

[1] Sangermano, Fr. Vicenzo, The Burmese Empire A Hundred Years Ago (1833)(3rd. ed. 1893)

than $500 to produce, but at government auction sells for $126,000. An estimated 43,000 tons were mined in 2011, but 21,000 tons were unaccounted for.

The following laws relate to the mining sector:
- Myanmar Mines Law 1994
- Myanmar Gemstone Law 1995
- Myanmar Mines Rules 1996

A foreign investor can apply to the Ministry of Mines in order to obtain a permit under the following categories:
- prospecting, exploration, large scale production or small scale production of metallic minerals;
- large-scale production of industrial minerals; or
- large-scale production of stone (decorative stones).

A company interested in mining must send a letter of interest to Ministry of Mines through its own national embassy. A technical discussion will be had with ministry, followed by a site visit. Documents required are a recommendation letter from the embassy, a letter of undertaking, a site visit schedule and passport copies to be submitted to the Ministry two weeks in advance. Then a formal proposal must be made to the Ministry of Mines, with copies to all relevant departments. Prospecting, exploration and feasibility studies are the responsibility of the Department of Geological Survey and Mineral Exploration of the Ministry. Mining rights are usually granted in the form of production sharing contracts or profit sharing concessions. After review, if approval is granted the documentation is sent to the Myanmar Investment Commission for consideration of the investment license.[2]

---

[2]Much of the text of this section is taken from Myanmar Legal Service's monograph, *Doing Business in Myanmar*, dated 9 September 2015.

CHAPTER 14

Oil and Gas

OIL PRODUCTION IN MYANMAR IS MORE than 1000 years old and the production is full of rich history and traditions:

> "Near Yay-nan-gyoung, in the petroleum district, when a new oil-well is wanted, the workmen place a marble image of an elephant on a smooth, flat stone, and surround it with gifts of all kinds, and then sit down to watch. If the elephant itself moves it indicates the direction in which borings are to be made; if not, the offering on which its shadow first falls as the sun sinks down, is marked, and a *baydin sayah* consulted."[1]

The Burmah Oil Company was successful in colonial Burma in the 19th century. By 1833 Burma was

---

[1] Scott, James George, Sir, The Burman, His Life and Notions (London) 1882

already exporting petroleum to Bengal. The company discovered the Yenangyaung oil field in 1887 and it is still producing today. Over time and due to mergers and acquisitions, Burmah Oil became a part of the Anglo-Persian Oil Company, which today is known as British Petroleum.

One of the causes of the Second World War in the Pacific was the American embargo preventing oil exports to Japan. Japan invaded Burma the day after Pearl Harbor in an effort to access Burmese oil. Myanmar has proven oil reserves of 2.1 billion barrels and production is 20,790 b/d.

The following laws relate to the oil and gas matters:
- The Oilfields Act (1918)
- The Oilfields Rules (1936)
- The Petroleum Act (1934)
- The Petroleum Rules (1937)
- The Essential Supplies and Services Act (Law No. 13/2012)
- The Water Power Act (1927)
- The Petroleum Resources (Development Regulation) Act (1957)
- The Law Amending the Petroleum Resources (Development Regulation) Act (1969)
- The Oilfield (Workers and Welfare) Act (1951)
- The Myanmar Petroleum Concession Rules (1962)

The Ministry of Energy is the primary governmental agency responsible for the oil and gas sector.

The state owned Myanma Oil and Gas Enterprise (MOGE) has the exclusive right to carry out all oil and gas operations with private contractors. The Ministry of Energy has sought to partner with multinationals in order to finance increased exploration and production in cooperation with Myanmar Oil and Gas Enterprise (MOGE) on a production-sharing basis. The Ministry of Energy will negotiate production-sharing contracts with foreign oil companies. Investors should expect to enter into either a production-sharing contract or an Improved Petroleum Recovery Contract with MOGE when investing in an oil and gas project. Currently, there are 17 onshore blocks and 20 offshore blocks in production.

Over 150 companies were registered with MOGE to serve as local partners for foreign oil companies or oilfield service companies. Bidders should partner with a Myanmar nationally-owned company. There are 26 blocks offshore and 47 onshore currently available for bid. Many of these available blocks are in the northeast of the country in the area between India and China. A local partner is mandatory for onshore and shallow water blocks, but optional for deep-water blocks.

On July 9, 2011 an auction for onshore blocks was held, resulting in the award of ten blocks to eight companies in 2012. Eighteen additional onshore blocks were auctioned in January, 2013 resulting in the award of 16 blocks to 11 companies in 2013. In 2014, an additional twenty blocks were awarded to thirteen companies.

Other opportunities in the oil and gas sector for foreign companies include research and development; rehabilitating older or declining fields; the construction of refineries for LPG, LNG or fertilizer; supplying floating storage and offtake facilities; CNG refueling stations and the marketing and retailing of petroleum products and supplying drilling rigs, refineries and plants.

Myanmar is 37th in the world in natural gas reserves and is expected to become a major producer. Proven reserves are at 25 trillion cubic feet (tcf). The offshore Yadana (Total, Chevron and PTTEP) and Yetagun (Petronas, PTTEP) natural gas projects started production in 1998 and 2000 respectively under gas sales contracts to the Thai state oil company PTT.

The Daewoo natural gas project started production in June 2013. The offshore Zawtika (PTTEP) natural gas project commenced production in March, 2014. Gas production and exports should increase when the Shwe and Zawtika gas fields and pipelines to China are completed. A 12.5% royalty is payable on production.

CHAPTER 15

Land Law

IN ANCIENT BURMA, A MAN'S HOUSE was determined by his station in life. Except for noblemen, houses were one story high. Houses were made of wood. Brick was forbidden, to prevent the house from being used as a fortress. Houses were always shaped like a tent. The house would stand on posts, so that the floor is seven or eight feet from the ground and usually consisted of one room or two rooms. In front of the house there would be a veranda, three or four feet lower than the general level of the house.

Under the 2008 Constitution, the Union is the ultimate owner of all land and natural resources. The right to hold private property is recognized by Article 37(c) and 372 of the Constitution. Article 356 obligates the Union to protect the lawfully acquired property of citizens. Under Myanmar law, both freehold and leasehold property rights are recognized. Title to land must be registered to be effective. After the colonial period, land could be acquired only through a system of grants typically for 60 or 90 years. Such a grant of land is alienable and divisible.

By 1865 offices for the registry of deeds were established in all towns where there was a resident judicial officer. Deeds could be filed in either the Burmese or English language. Mortgages were to be recorded and, if not paid, foreclosed upon by a judicial proceeding. If a mortgagee held his land for twelve years without the mortgagor taking action, the mortgagor could no longer bring suit on the mortgage. Today, unfortunately, there is no national property register. The lack of a clear title system has made due diligence investigations of ownership a daunting though necessary task.

Despite these general laws, there is no single land law in Myanmar. There are different laws relating to different types of land such as forestlands, farmland, undeveloped land and industrial estates. Freehold is reserved exclusively for Burmese nationals. In the absence of title, ownership is recognized in ancestral lands. This is not a theoretical or historical artifact: in a recent case, farmers sought to reclaim 600 acres taken by the government in 1986 as "ancestral lands". In another, farmers in the Sagain Region sought the restoration of farmland taken without compensation by the Burmese Army in 1996. In a ceremony on April 11, 2014, the land was returned to the farmers.

The Transfer of Immovable Property Restriction Act of 1987 prohibits the sale or transfer of land to foreigners or foreign companies. Foreign interests may only lease land for a period of up to one year unless exempted by the government. Such an exemption can be obtained under the authority of a license granted under the Foreign Investment Law permitting a lease for up to 50 years with two possible renewable terms of ten years each. A longer renewal period is possible in underdeveloped areas. There is currently an adjustment period as the Registrar of Deeds modifies his procedures to be able to register leases to foreign entities authorized by the Foreign Investment law.

As of 2011, one-third of the population lives in urban areas. This is expected to increase at the rate of 2.5% per annum.

A minimal real estate tax is imposed by the municipal authorities. Stamp duty for transactions denominated in Myanmar kyats is as follows:

- 5% on sale of property plus additional 2% on Yangon property.
- .3% share transfers.
- 2% on bond transfers
- 2% on estates

For transactions denominated in other currencies a 1% rate applies.

The applicability of the term "condominium"in Burmese law is restricted to apartments in elevator buildings at least eight stories high. There are height restrictions on buildings in Yangon to insure that buildings are not built taller than the Schwedagon Pagoda, which is 326 feet high. Some use nominees to avoid restrictions but this makes enforcement of rights impossible if the cooperation of the nominee is lost.

The new condominium law was passed in January, 2016 allowing foreigners to buy up to 40

The real property market functions as a brake on the country's foreign investment plans. Because of high land prices, for small and medium-sized companies the cost of entering the market are prohibitive. Because the financing of real estate ventures is limited, demand in every sector is greater than supply. As of March 2014, in Yangon vacant Class A office space is essentially nonexistent. Several companies offer serviced offices. Nevertheless, the Yangon City Development Committee is promoting new projects in Yangon. Because of the congestion in Rangoon's city center, new companies often rent and convert villas to offices. Zoning and urban planning are haphazard. There is no current scheme for licensing architects.

Where a foreign company seeks to rent land, Directive No. 3/90 applies. This rule provides that construction of new buildings in downtown areas shall not exceed six stories and annual lease rates should be in accord with commercial rates. Government entities may lease land for thirty years on a BOT (build, operate and transfer) basis. With the approval of the Government and the Myanmar Investment Commission the period may be extended. Prior approval is required for subleases. Rent for the lease will be periodically reviewed and the lessee obtains no rights to resources found in, on or under leased land.

Real property lease agreements must contain the following terms and conditions:

- Specify the purpose of land use clearly;
- An undertaking by the lessee to comply with the laws of Myanmar;
- Lease term of less than thirty years (unless greater term granted by the MIC);
- Optional provision providing for lease extension negotiations prior to close of thirty year period;
- Review of lease rate every five years;
- Post-construction lease rate review every five years after construction completion;
- New lease rates to be at future market rates at time of review;
- Ten percent discount for paying five years' rental in advance;
- Termination of lease for breach of contract if {unauthorized} buildings on land;
- Prior government approval required for subleasing, mortgaging and right to occupy premises;
- Lessee acquires no ownership right in any newly discovered natural resources.

Moe Thida, assistant Director at the Ministry of Constructions Department of Human Settlement and Housing Development, admitted that there are many challenges:

"We lack an integrated urban plan, a
land use plan, a housing plan, and an urban services plan [and that may] hinder
the proper housing development. We lack
the legal basis for the government to moni-
tor and intervene in unused and underused
land, unoccupied and incomplete buildings, to justify the sales price of private
developers."[1]

For many years there were restrictions on the importation of automobiles. The restrictions have been lifted
and new vehicles have been added to the roads, adding
to this congestion. To complicate matters, nation-wide
only 20% of the roads are paved.

There is a special regime for farmland. On March
30, 2012 the Farmland Law (Law No. 2/2012) was
passed. The law recognizes the State as the owner of
all lands but grants land use certificates to farmers.
The Township Farmland Management Body has the
responsibility to issue certificates at the local level,
and attention is paid to rights a farmer may have by
virtue of inheritance or acquisition. Ownership lies is
somewhere between a freehold and a trust. That is, the
farmers by virtue of inheritance, acquisition or lease
may farm lands with the approval of the government,
who is considered the ultimate owner. Farmers may

---

[1]As reported by Khine Kyaw in *Myanmar Eleven*, "Rapid
Urbanisation requires Solutions".

alienate property for which they hold a certificate to farm and may pass such farmed land to their heirs. Provisions are made for the compensation of farmers in cases of eminent domain. The law revokes the 1953 Land Nationalization Act, the 1963 Disposal of Tenancies Law and the 1963 Farmer's Rights Protection Law.

Environmental Law

Environmental law as a subject separate from common law nuisance or trespass is a creature of the 20th century. In Myanmar there were no separate statutory environmental laws other than those handed down or developed under the common law until the 2008 Constitution which guaranteed the conservation of natural resources and promoted the preservation of the environment.

The Environmental Conservation Law (Law No. 9/2012) was passed on March 30, 2012. Environmental protection now falls under the jurisdiction of the National Commission for Environmental Affairs. The Commission is responsible for setting environmental standards. The Commission monitors acts of other government agencies that might harm the environment and intervenes if necessary and to carry out Union environmental policies. The law provides for the establishment of standards as to water safety, air quality, noise and emissions, fluid waste and any other necessary quality standards. Conservation of natural resources is declared to be a policy of the government. Environmental impact statements (called, "prior permissions") are required for projects as well as insurance in case of accidents or spills.

An earlier law, the Conservation of Water Resources and Rivers Law (Law No. 8/2006) prohibited the unauthorized discharge of toxic chemicals into the nation's waterways. While the administrative procedures under that law have been superseded by the Environmental Conservation Law, the Conservation Law's specific provisions continue to have relevance.

Environmental Conservation Law Rules were enacted on June 5, 2014. The Ministry is given the authority to draft procedures and implement the National Environmental Policy.

CHAPTER 16

Capital Markets

THE SECURITIES EXCHANGE LAW OF 2013 provided for the creation of both a a fully-functional stock market exchange and regulator by 2015. The previous stock exchange was closed by the military government in 1962. The new exchange, the Yangon Stock Exchange, is a joint venture between Myanmar and Japan and opened in April, 2016. There is yet no continuous trading, but instead two daily auctions are held.

In the region, the Viet Nam bourse has been successful while Cambodia and Laos have lagged behind. With less than five companies traded, there is not yet sufficient momentum in Myanmar for the Yangon Exchange to achieve critical mass.

Companies wishing to list must demonstrate two years of profitability and a minimum of 100 shareholders. At the time of writing, only three companies are listed. The First Private Bank is scheduled to be the fourth listed company on the exchange. There are five licensed brokerage firms.

Foreign investors are not yet permitted access to the market but new legislation is anticipated whcih will permit foreign investors to buy and sell securities. The purchase of shares is a non-traditional method of capital preservation in Myanmar. Historically, asset preservation was accomplished by hoarding gold. Officials of the Exchange are engaged in a mission to educate the public about the advantages, as well as the pitfalls, of purchasing securities.

If foreigners are permitted to purchase shares than the novelty aspect of the Yangon Stock Exchange will be lessened. The risk is that the share-buying public— initially, a small group in Myanmar—will assume that subsequently listing less-strong companies will yield profits. The first company traded on the Exchange, First Myanmar Investment, owned by real estate tycoon Serge Pun, opened at $31 per share and as of November, 2016, is trading at only $12 per share. With thin trading and few IPO's, Myanmar has been spared the enthusiasm seen in other countries.

Nevertheless, there is an opportunity for experienced law firms to assist companies in going public. There is also an opportunity to assist in the licensing of brokers and dealers for the exchange. To the extent that the regulations remain unwritten, opportunities exist in shaping and molding the regulatory environment so that the Exchange will be successful.

CHAPTER 17

Intellectual Property

DRAFT INTELLECTUAL PROPERTY laws will bring Myanmar in line with world IP protection standards. These laws are already in written form and may be enacted at any time. Until then, however, Myanmar's legislative protection of intellectual property is accomplished through a collection of mostly historical laws. The most recent copyright legislation is the Copyright Law of 1924. Protection exists only for original works if first published in Myanmar or if the author is a Myanmar citizen at the time of creation. The 2008 Constitution recognizes the "right of private invention and patent"in Article 372. One of the basic principles as stated in the Constitution's Article 37(c) is a recognition of patent according to law.

In the absence of a trademark law, trademark owners can file a Declaration of Ownership with the Yangon Registration Office of the Settlement and Land Records Department. The filing should show use of the mark in Myanmar. This filing is considered prima facie trademark ownership. Notices are also customarily published in newspapers, at least once every three years.

The Patent and Design Act 1939 was repealed by the Patent and Design (Emergency Provisions) Act 1946. These laws were repealed in 1993 and not replaced. A patent may nevertheless be registered in the Register of Deeds. There is no special legislation relating to trade secrets other than those torts recognized by the common law such as theft and conversion.

A new comprehensive intellectual property law is anticipated. The current collection of laws does not meet WTO requirements, though according to the government, Myanmar is implement WTO requirements "as per schedule."Myanmar is not a signatory to the Berne Convention. Because of its WTO membership, Myanmar automatically became a member of the Agreement on Trade-Related Aspects of Intellectual Property Rights ("TRIPS") as of 1 January 1995.

The absence of legislative action does not necessarily mean that rights owners are without remedies. Given the recognition of patents, private invention and the like in the Constitution, coupled with the courts' ability to issue writs, including injunctive relief, there is at least arguably a basis to protect intellectual property rights on a common law using solely judicial remedies. Article 296 sets forth the writs available to the Supreme Court of Myanmar, but Article 378(b) provides that the identification of such writs is not in derogation of any powers lower courts might have to issue writs under existing law.

Enforcement then, is a question of framing violations in terms of historic common law causes of action. While the issue of whether there exists common-law copyright outside of legislation is one of some controversy there is no reason why common law tort actions for theft or misappropriation could not be used in the absence of legislation, whether in the area of copyright, patents, trademarks or trade secrets. Thus, an owner of intellectual property may apply for a permanent injunction against theft, infringement or misuse, though as in the case of any other kind of litigation, results may be unpredictable.

CHAPTER 18

Corruption

IN THE EARLY 20TH CENTURY, CORRUPTION was a way of life in Burma. The police were available for hire and local officials were known to sue in court if their promised bribes were not paid.

In this environment, though the Indian Criminal Code applied, what constituted misconduct on the frontier was not always well defined. Burma had a system of *myo-oks*, or miniature monarchs, to whom patronage was owed. The British believed these officials were entirely corrupt.

With this background in mind, the Union Government drafted and passed an Anti-Corruption Law that took effect in August 2011. The law established a Commission for the Eradication of Bribery. The Commission can require asset reporting by officials; seize evidence, freeze properties, investigate bank accounts and forfeit illicit riches. The law applies to both public officials and individuals who aid and abet corrupt behavior.

For U.S. persons, United States law may apply. The phrase, "U.S. person" is a term of art and includes not only U.S. corporations, but anyone holding a U.S. resident visa. Under the "effects"test, "[t]he anti-fraud laws of the United States—of which anti-corruption legislation is but one—may be given extraterritorial reach whenever a predominantly foreign transaction has substantial effects within the United States."*Consol. Gold Fields PLC v. Minorco, S.A.*, 871 F.2d 252, 261-62 (2d Cir.1989). This test is met where the domestic effect is "a direct and foreseeable result of the conduct outside of the United States."*Id.* at 262.

18.1 Elimination of Sanctions

On October 7, 2016, President Obama signed an Executive Order which revoked U.S. economic sanctions against Myanmar. This Executive Order was the result of a meeting between Aung San Suu Kyi and the president. According to a an official press release, the United States government believes that in light of Myanmar's election of a "civilian-led, democratically elected government,"the removal of economic sanctions will promote Myanmar's growth. On the same day, the federal Financial Crimes Enforcement Network (FinCEN) announced that in line with the Executive Order, financial institutions would be permitted to maintain correspondent accounts for Myanmar banks.

The revocation is wide ranging. Its effects initially are as follows:

- All individuals and entities blocked pursuant to the Burmese Sanctions Regulations (BSR) have been removed from OFACs Specially Designated Nationals and Blocked Persons (SDN) List.
- All property and interests in property blocked pursuant to the BSR are unblocked.
- The ban on the importation into the United States of Burmese-origin jadeite and rubies, and any jewelry containing them, has been revoked.
- All OFAC-administered restrictions under the Burma sanctions program regarding banking or financial transactions with Burma are no longer in effect.
- OFAC will remove the BSR from the Code of Federal Regulations.
- Compliance with the State Departments Responsible Investment Reporting Requirements is no longer required by OFACs regulations and is now voluntary. [1]

Anti-narcotics measures against specified individuals remain in effect. Transactions with or involving those identified as Specially Designated Nationals under other laws continue to be prohibited. It is also a

---

[1]Source: U.S. Treasury Department, Office of Public Affairs, "Treasury Implements Termination of Burma Sanctions Program,"(October 7, 2016)

crime to "facilitate" a transaction with a Specially Designated National. It is not clear whether or not the crime of facilitation will incur additional penalties, since the general American aiding and abetting statute provides for punishment as a principal.

Nevertheless, it is possible to request a license for a particular transaction.If OFAC's handling of Cuba licenses is any lesson, these licenses will not be impossible to get. The U.S. government further retains jurisdiction to prosecute anyone who violated the sanctions when they were in force. However, the U.S. Treasury Department's Office of Foreign Assets Control (OFAC) had issued License #17 under the Burmese Sanctions Regulations on July 11, 2012. The license permitted U.S. persons to invest in Myanmar generally.

The cumulative effect of the elimination of U.S. sanctions is to open Myanmar to American business, commerce and trade.

European Community trade and financial sanctions against Myanmar were terminated in April, 2013. The EU continues to maintain restrictions on the sale of arms to Myanmar that could be used for internal repression. The arms embargo is set to expire in April, 2017. The American elimination of sanctions contains no restrictions on trade in weapons other than the existing non-country specific requirement to obtain licenses for the export sale of arms. Canada and Australia removed all sanctions except for arms exports.

Chapter 19

APPENDIX

19.0.1 BRITISH GOVERNMENT AD-VICE TO SOLDIERS, 1945

1. The Burmese peoples are our friends. Most of the hill peoples have been engaged in active guerilla warfare against the Japs since 1942, and many thousands of plains-people have given us help at the risk of their lives. Show them you appreciate what they have done.

2. As a nation the Burmese are more polite than we are. Try to remember the special terms of respect for elderly people and local officials.

3. Always work through the local officials, especially the headmen in Burmese villages and the chiefs in hill villages. They are "big shots"in their own little world, and can smooth your way a lot.

4. Treat Burmese women with great respect. They live a much freer life than most Eastern women, but

their smile doesn't mean they want to go to bed with you.

5. Remember that a laugh will take you a long way farther than a frown.

6. Wear your clothing loose if you want to avoid heat-stroke (this is not to say you should appear sloppily dressed when out of the battle area).

7. Doctor all cuts and scratches at once.

8. Take extra salt in your drinking water.

9. The Japanese made enormous capital out of the relatively small fifth column they used in 1942. Don't help them now by believing every Burmese is against us.

10. Don't get mixed up with political or religious discussions with the Burmese. They have plenty of trouble for themselves without our butting in.

11. Don't laugh at what you see at festivals. Very often there is a religious significance in these and your derision will give deep offense.

12. Don't gamble with the Burmese.

13. Don't get drawn into arguments about the relative merits of United Nations forces operating on the Burma front.

14. Don't let yourself get bitten by bugs and mosquitoes more than you can help. Follow the precautionary drill.

15. Don't drink unsterilized water.

16. Don't eat native foods sold in the bazaars.

17. Don't eat raw vegetables.

18. Don't eat raw fruit unless it's the sort you can peel.

19. Don't meddle with pagodas and shrines. Even though they are allowed to fall into ruin they are still held in veneration.

20. Don't shoot animals or bird near sacred places.

21. Don't photograph people without asking for their permission, and don't start a racket by paying for permission.

HOTELS

Finding inexpensive to luxury accommodation is no longer a problem in Yangon. The list below was compiled in those days when finding accommodation was still an issue. Rather than update the list, a quick check on TripAdvisor will yield the names of appropriate hotels for the business traveler.

3-4 Stars

Hotel Equatorial 33, Alan Pya Pagoda Road, Dagon P.O., Yangon, Tel: 250388 Fax 951-252478

Hotel Nikko Royal Lake Yangon 40, Natmauk Road Tarmway P.O., Yangon T: 544500, Fax: 951-544400

Kandawgyi Palace Hotel Kan Yeik Tha Road, Yangon, Tel. 249-255,6,7,8,9; Fax: 951-280412/242766

Nawarat Concorde Hotel 257, Insein Road, Oakkyin P.O., Yangon, 667-888, 667-777

Inya Lake Hotel Kaba Aye Pagoda Road, Yangon, 662-857, 662-858 (formerly the New World Inya Lake Hotel)

Pansea Hotel 35, Taw Win Road, Dagon P.O., Yangon, 221-462, 228-260

Ramada Hotel Yangon International Airport, 666-979, 666-699

Savoy Hotel 129, Dhammazedi Road, Bahan P.O., Yangon 526-289, 526-298

Sedona Hotel No. 1, Kaba Aye Pagoda Road, Yankin P.O., 666-900, 666-911

Strand, The, 92 Strand Road, 281-553, 281-534, Fax 951-289-880

Summit Parkview Hotel, 350 Ahlone Road, Dagon P.O., 227-966 Fax 951-227-992

Traders Hotel, 223 Sule Pagoda Rd., Kyauktada t. 242-828/f.951-242-834

1-2 Stars

Bagan Inn 29, Natmauk Lane 2, Po Sein Road, Tamwe P.O. Tel. 550-489/548-148 Fax: 951-549-600

Hotel December 89(A) Pyay Road, Dagon P.O., Yangon Myanmar, 221-943, Fax 951-289-960

Hotel Windsor 31, Shin Saw Pu Street, Sanchaung P.O., 510-037/247-718, F. 951-511-218

Yoma Hotel No. 146 Bogyoke Aung San Street, 297-725/297-726 Fax: 951-297-957, 297-958

Yoma Hotel II, No. 24-A, Inya Road, Kamayut P.O., t. 531-065/525-48

SOURCES

BOOKS

Bixby, Olive Jenny, *My Child-Life in Burmah, or Recollections and Incidents*,(Boston, 1880)

British Army, *A Pocket Guide to Burma*, (1945)

CIA World Factbook 2013

Ezdani Yvonne Vaz, *Songs of the Survivors*, Goa 1556 Publishers, Goa, 2007

Forbes, Capt. C.J.F.S., *Legendary History of Burma and Arakan*, Rangoon 1882

Fryer, Capt. George Edward, *Handbook of British Burma*, Maulmein, 1867;

Greenwood, Nicholas, *Shades of Gold and Green, Anecdotes of Colonial Burmah, 1886-1948*, Asian Educational Services, 1998

Griffin, Andrew, *A Brief Guide to Sources for the Study of Burma in the India Office Records*, India Office Library and Records (London, 1979),

Larkin, Emma, *Finding George Orwell in Burma*, Penguin, 2004, 2011

Myint-U, Thant, *The River of Lost Footsteps*, Farrar Strauss Giroux 2006, 2008

O'Brien, Harriett, *Forgotten Land, A Rediscovery of Burma,* (Penguin, London 1991)

Pantoja-Hidalgo, Cristina, *Five Years in a Forgotten Land: A Burmese Notebook*, University of the Philippines Press, Quezon City 1991

Saha, Jonathan, Law, *Disorder and the Colonial State: Corruption in Burma c. 1900*, Palgrave Macmillan (London) 2013

Sangermano, Fr. Vincenzo, *The Burmese Empire A Hundred Years Ago*, {*Description of the Burmese Empire*}(1833), 3d ed. 1898.

Scott, James George, Sir, *The Burman, his life and notions,* London, Macmillan and Co. 1882

Whisenhut, Donald, *President Herbert Hoover*, New York, Nova Publishers 2007

Reports

"Finance: Myanmar Update", VDB-Loi (Law Firm), Yangon, 2016

"GAO Report to Congressional Committees: International Trade US Agencies have taken Some Steps, but Serious Impediments Remain to Restricting Trade in Burmese Rubies and Jadeite"(2009)

"Myanmar Business Guide", Price Waterhouse Cooper November 13, 2013

"Myanmar Country Report 2013", The Economist Intelligence Unit

"Myanmar Investment Guide 2013", Myanmar Investment Commission

"Myanmar Oil and Gas Sector", presented in Yangon in February, 2014, Albert T. Chandler & Daw Khin Cho Kyi, Managing Partner, Myanmar Legal Services Ltd.

"The Report: Myanmar 2014", Oxford Business Group

News Media

"Burma's Superstitious Rulers", Andrew Seith, *The Interpreter*, October 22, 2009, http://www.lowyinterpreter.org/post/2009/10/22/Burmas-superstitious-leaders.aspx

"Getting Ready for the Major League", Nyeinchan Win and Thet Mon Htun, *Eleven Media* (Myanmar) December 13, 2013

"The Land of Courtesy and Colour", A. Claude Brown (1927), reprinted in *Shades of Gold and Green, supra.*

"Myanmar: What the World is Reading", Special Report of *The Nation*, (newspaper) Bangkok, March 27, 2014.

"Myanmar Fortune Teller Predicts End to Crisis", *The Nation*, March 1, 2014

"Myanmar Poised to Become New Mining Mecca for Chinese Investors", Cecilia Jamasmie, October 25, 2012, retrieved from http://www.mining.com/myanmar-poised-to-become-new-mining-mecca-for-chinese-investors-44189/

"Myanmar to Review Existing Mining and Energy Contracts", Cecilia Jamasmie, April 12, 2013, retrieved from http://www.mining.com
/myanmar-to-review-existing-mining-and-energy-contracts-29745/

"Rangoon, 1941"(1947), Silvia Baker, reprinted in *Shades of Gold and Green, supra.*

"Tatmadaw Returns Confiscated Land to Sagaing Farmers", Hlaing Kyaw Soe, *Myanmar Times*, April 24, 2014

Cases and Legal Articles

"A New Arbitration Law for Myanmar", Katrina Limond, Allen and Overy, http://www.allenovery.com/publications/en-gb/Pages/A-new-arbitration-law-for-Myanmar.aspx
Burma Sanctions, USG (General): http://www.treasury.gov/resource-center/sanctions/Programs/Documents/burmagl18.pdf

Burma Sanctions, USG, Executive Order: http://www.whitehouse.gov/the-press-office/2013/08/07/executive-order-prohibiting-certain-imports-burmese-jadeite-and-rubies

"Case Note: Comparative Law Aspects of the *Doe v. Unocal* Choice of Law Hearing", Andrew Huxley, *Journal of Comparative Law* 1:1 (2006) 219.

Doe v. Unocal, 395 F.3d 932 (9th Cir. 2002); *vacated* 403 F.3d 708 (9th Cir. 2005)

"Golden Land: Protecting Investments in Myanmar from Disputes", John Lichtfield, Kyaw Zin Htet, April 3, 2014, retrieved from http://www.globallegalpost.com/blogs/global-view/golden-land-protecting-investments-in-myanmar-from-disputes-95192130/

"Legal Education in Burma since the 1960s"[unpublished version] Myint Zan, longer version of article written for the *Journal of Burma Studies*, v. 12 (2008)

"The Rule of Law and Commercial Litigation in Myanmar", Alec Christie, 10 *Pacific Rim Law & Policy Jrnl.* (No. 1) p.47 (2000)

"The Rule of Law in Myanmar: Challenges and Prospects", Report of the International Bar Association's Human Rights Institute (2012)

Rules of Practice for the Better Regulation of Cases Referred to Arbitration, dated 18 July 1861

U.S. Treasury Department, Office of Public Affairs, "Treasury Implements Termination of Burma Sanctions Program,"(October 7, 2016)

19.1 Myanmar Foreign Investment Government Offices

DIRECTORATE OF INVESTMENT AND COMPANY ADMINISTRATION
www.dica.gov.mm/index.htm

FOR COMPANY REGISTRATION:
COMPANY REGISTRATION OFFICE
DIRECTORATE OF INVESTMENT AND COMPANY ADMINISTRATION
MINISTRY OF NATIONAL PLANNING AND ECONOMIC DEVELOPMENT
Building No.1, ThitSar Road, Yankin Township
Yangon, Myanmar
Tel: +95-1-657891. Fax: +95-1-657825
Website: www.mnped.gov.mm/index.php

FOR EXPORT & IMPORT:
EXPORT IMPORT REGISTRATION OFFICE
DIRECTORATE OF TRADE MINISTRY OF COMMERCE
Building No. 3
Nay Pyi Taw, Myanmar
Tel: +95-67-408009; 406124; 408003
Fax: +95-67-408234
Website: www.commerce.gov.mm
DIRECTORATE OF TRADE
YANGON BRANCH

No. 226/240, Strand Road
Pabedan Township
Yangon Myanmar
Tel: +95-1-251197
Fax: +95-1-253028

**FEDERATION OF CHAMBERS OF COM-
MERCE AND INDUSTRY (UMFCCI)**
No.29, Min Ye Kyawswa Road
Lanmadaw Township
Yangon, Myanmar
Tel: +95-1-214344, 214345, 214346, 214347, 214348,
214349
Fax: +95-1-214484
Website: www.umfcci.com.mm
www.umfcci.net
Email: umcci@mptmail.net.mm

CHAPTER 20

About the Author

MICHAEL O'KANE IS AN AMERICAN-TRAINED attorney with more than a decade's experience overseas. He is a former special legal advisor to the Kingdom of Saudi Arabia and in that capacity drafted a legal code for the Kingdoms Economic Cities project. His book, *Doing Business in Saudi Arabia* has reached #20 on Amazons International Law bestseller list. He has also written three other books on Saudi law, including *Saudi Labor Law Outline*, *Saudi Securities Law* and *Saudi Real Property Law and Practice*.

All these books are available from Amazon, Barnes & Noble and iTunes.

Index